The Mostly True Stories

of Dr. Juan Harrison

Linda
Hope you enjoy
it.
Juan Harrison

Dedication

I thank my late mother for her love of learning and her burning desire for me to be the first one in the family to graduate college. Praises go to my wife for putting up with my constant scribbling and leaving potential titles on envelopes lying around. I'm especially grateful for my wife Sheri typing my weekly posts which spares me from enduring the almost excruciating pain of sitting down at the keyboard. A special note of gratitude goes to my eldest son Ryan who got me started writing after I retired and my youngest son Clay who set me up on these weekly posts and endeavors to keep me on good terms with Facebook. As published authors they have encouraged me to put my thoughts in print, so I give them all the credit or blame. Finally, thanks to all my faithful followers who encourage me with their supportive reactions and make me feel a part of a larger family through my weekly Facebook posts.

Preface

I did not plan to be a writer. Mostly, I'm a talker. However, one son pulled me into writing Serving Happiness in 2015 and Class Rules in 2016 as I was doing written, audio, and video presentations called "Looking up with Dr. Juan Harrison." I finally got out of that as my eldest got too busy to manage my online activities. Part 2 arrived in the form of Dr. Juan Harrison.com on Facebook after I agreed to start writing weekly posts in 2018 if my youngest won his Judge race. He did so I did.

All earlier writings and my weekly posts are and have been geared toward encouraging others, especially the elderly, as we face the daily challenges of loneliness, loss of spouse, adapting to change, coping with family relationships and the list goes on. I want the reader to feel that she is not alone. I undergird my thoughts with encouragement to develop a strong personal faith that will help a person through the hard times when we often feel alone and almost defeated.

For me, I love the reactions and responses that readers and followers share back with me and other readers. By creating a sense of community I often get to sit back and let readers give us great testimonies of faith as they have endured hardships and received blessings. As a Sunday school teacher for 60 years I've learned, especially with seniors, the importance of letting each class member share praises and burdens even if it means I have little time to teach. By our age if we haven't gotten a good understanding of the scriptures it may be we're not likely to acquire much more understanding. What I do see is the need to be listened to and to share thoughts with other human beings.

I hope that others who have not seen my stories and posts about discovering what really matters in life will take them as a challenge to help find ways to bring peace, joy, and happiness into their lives. To grow old and not gain the wisdom of what is most important in life is a sad situation. Hopefully my readers can discover that true happiness comes from serving others, while only serving self leads to misery and frustration.

Readers, thank you for your valuable time. May you feel it's been worth it to take a few moments to find out how other struggling pilgrims are trying to make their way through a world growing more challenging each day. May you find encouragement as we share what helps us through life

Lucky

I bent down beneath the drive-thru window of a business customer of mine and found a penny. Made my day. Today I stepped out of my car at a convenience store and there was this neat trail of eight pennies right at my feet. Holy Toledo! This may sound juvenile to you, but I look for pennies or dimes or nickels lying around. Maybe it goes with my attitude toward business. I always told my boys to not look at a yard as grass to be mowed but rather money lying there waiting for them to pick it up.

I'm not a generally lucky guy. I've been blessed way beyond what I deserve, but I'm not all that lucky. My wife has the touch; I don't. I may be the dumb one. I guess I always figured I kinda made my own luck. I've always heard that the harder I work, the luckier I get. Once I won three dollars on something and almost had cardiac arrest. My total lifetime winnings up to that point had been an Evergreen feed cap at a livestock show. If the prize patrol ever came to my house, I'm not sure how dependable my Depends might be. On the other hand, I did find my wife at a Rangers ballgame, so I can't say luck totally passed me by.

You get the PCH envelope. Do you throw it away, or do you fill it out making sure your magical winning number is showing through the envelope. For the forty second consecutive year they remind you that you did not order a magazine or a magic skillet that will not stick. Why do you persist? It is because you know if you don't enter you have zero chance to win. If you do enter, it's down to a few million to one. You know you're an optimist when you keep licking that stamp and sending it in.

I'm not even going to mention the guy or gal that plops a dollar down twice a week just to have the pleasure of having the little machine giggle and print out, "Not a winner."

I take offense that some machine would have the gall to tell me I'm not a winner. What it doesn't know is that I really am a winner. When you add up great family, friends, fun retirement, reasonable health, and all bills paid up, I'd say I'm a lucky guy, or maybe I'd say the machine is wrong. I won the lottery when I was fortunate enough to be born a Texan in a great land. I didn't deserve it one bit. Just to breathe in the air of freedom and take in the sweet tasting nectar of opportunity makes me one of the luckiest and most blessed winners of all.

Contact

A while back I saw an independent Christian film where two teenage brothers pretty much raised themselves; the father abdicated his role as he spent his time grieving for his late wife and drinking her memory away. The boys paid the price. Thankfully a grandmotherly neighbor lady who could not have children stepped in to fill the void left by the father. She made sure they had food and provided work for them at her local grocery store. Both sides benefitted; they now had someone to care for them and she now found a replacement for the children she never had.

Over the years I've known a number of childless couples. It often seems that they are some of the nicest people who would make great parents. Some adopt children; some become foster parents; some choose to not do either. The movie I mentioned reminded me that lemons into lemonade applies here.

There is a world of children and young people who could greatly benefit from a kind person willing to invest some time in the life of a child. I'll never forget the neighbor who played catch with me after my father left. Likewise the neighbor lady across the street helped me learn to love fishing as she took me along to half the ponds in the county.

In my lifetime I've been privileged to serve on Big Brother and Big Sister boards and local food bank boards where we helped get food to foster families. You don't have to be on some formal board to make a difference. There's a world of children and young people out there ready for someone to invest in their lives. We're taught that if we seek we will find. I've learned in life, be it used car, another job, a good friend, or an opportunity to serve others, God will send it our way if we are looking. He gives us the desires of our hearts and desires to bless us if we're ready. He has the answer before we know the question.

Something that has stood me in good stead in my life is that if I get a little down or am having a pity party as we're missing someone or not feeling very useful, just start seriously looking for an opportunity to serve or someone to care about and the blues will go away. Man was meant to care for one another. Being a selfish hermit is no good for anyone. Ask Scrooge. Before you know it you'll be getting back more than you could imagine.

Out of Sight

As we touched down onto the runway, chickens ran for their lives. The rundown buildings gave an image of a banana republic. Any moment now I expected to see Earnest Borgnine of <u>McHales Navy</u> come around the corner with his gap toothed grin.

Santa Maria is probably the smallest of the nine Azore archipelago islands. It is long and skinny. It belonged to Portugal a thousand miles away and sits four hours by air from England. The atmosphere here was that of a lazy tourist haven, albeit a poor one.

The climate I experienced there contrasted with the tense atmosphere in Cypress where we were asked to carry our own bags to the next plane. I sensed they didn't want them blowing up in their hands. It didn't help that we had just dodged explosions in the Golan Heights the day before.

What has impressed me as I have travelled has been the ability of people to adapt to whatever the situation is around them. In one small country I met people who paid half their salaries to support the government, primarily the army. Missiles frequently dropped over their borders. Young male and female soldiers patrol everywhere with automatic weapons. They live surrounded by enemies. At any time a missile could come crashing in on them. Still, they forge ahead leaning on centuries of survival in the face of overwhelming odds. They have the rare distinction of having had a historic past, surviving centuries of slavery, near annihilation in WWII and rising again to gather back together as a country. Every time I see my favorite play and movie, <u>Fiddler on the Roof,</u> I'm reminded of the hardships and nightmares people endured in different countries overseas.

Americans have been blessed in the last century to have avoided the destructive wars on our soil that have almost destroyed countries in places like Europe, Middle East, and Asia. We have graciously and generously provided materials and sacrificed patriotic souls to help fight the war on their lands.

As we have recently done in the Middle East, we have been willing to sacrifice human lives to protect our allies and hopefully keep wars away from our shores. Sometimes long distance conflicts cause us to forget that we could be the place of conflict instead of over there. It lets us forget or hardly be aware of what some Americans have volunteered to do to hopefully spare our land the scars of wars the last century or so. It's easy to become blasé and cynical, even to the point of not being willing to pay that price any more.

The old phrase "Pay me now, or pay me later," applies to cancer and war. In WWII the Allies almost waited too long to act. The terror attacks of 9/11 are reminders of what other people around the world endure on a daily basis. Sometimes it's good to travel a bit and be reminded what we have avoided and other countries have endured in recent times. We have made great sacrifices in recent world conflicts. The scars are not on our buildings or our lands; the scars are in the hearts and on the bodies of selfless ordinary American citizens willing to give all so that our homeland might not have to wear the same marks caused by recent wars on other shores.

Nothing On

How many times have I heard my wife say, "There's nothing on TV fit to watch." She's probably more right than wrong. Censorship or lack of it keeps letting the hand of morality slowly slide up the knee, up the leg of good taste toward the thigh of depravity. Now I'm hungry for fried chicken, legs and thighs.

My poor wife endures Fox News rattling on for a big part of the day. I may have it turned on in both ends of the house; you never know when that breaking news is going to reveal the latest scandal. My wife thinks it's all the same stuff being rehashed. We have a deal; I don't criticize her constant perusing of Facebook and all her friends' grandkids doing some boogie dance, and she won't fuss about me watching the same story repeated five hours in a row with each talking head trying to put a new spin on their version. If you're the unfortunate newscaster at the tail end of the story, you now know how it felt to be last in line on Saturday night before running water days. You got to finally dip into that dirty gray or sometimes almost black water. Good luck with that.

When you finally burn out on Fox News and the pretty blonde broadcasters, then I try my luck with <u>Gunsmoke, Mash, Little House, and Everybody Loves Raymond.</u> Before long you realize you've seen most of those. Maybe you give up and watch <u>Andy Griffith</u> for the twentieth time; you know you're in trouble when you've memorized the dialogue. It's still good stuff. It helps flush out the garbage that has run through your ears during the day. They call it the "News." I think it should be called the "Olds."

When all else fails I pick up a book my sons have given me about the decline of America or how to be a success. I'm afraid I'm going to have to settle for mediocre at this stage of my life. I'm not sure if I can have much effect on our country's snowball's rapid descent toward Hell. I'm hopeful, but not overly optimistic. For my kids and grandkids, I regret they didn't get to live in a time of close neighbors and strong families. Ozzie and Harriet used to live here.

Bottom line, I've read the Story and I know how it ends. I just pray for the faith to hang in there until the trumpet sounds.

Cheerleader

Over the years I've learned that there are more things I'm not good at versus what I am good at. When you look at the glass, is it half empty or half full? If you focus on your shortcomings, failures, and faults, you're in for a long, miserable life. In Christian terms I think the Devil routinely reminds us how undeserving and miserable creatures we are. He delights in reminding us of our past failures, broken promises to have and hold, and screw ups that make us feel defeated.

Fortunately we don't have to live there. It's a whole lot easier walking on the high road than in the mud. If we are lucky or blessed, we may find someone to help us up out of the sewer and muck of life and help plant our feet on solid ground. My book Class Rules might help someone you know get started on building a new life based on solid fundamentals. For a lot of us that influence was a faithful mom or humble father who showed us how to live. You can throw in some aunts, grandmas, and other loving relatives. Maybe you didn't have much family help, but an outsider took an interest in you. James tells us we are "to look after orphans and widows in their distress." Psalms promises "a father to the fatherless, a defender of widows, is God in his holy dwelling."

It is easy to feel abandoned and neglected in this life. But if we believe the Word, we accept that He will be a father to the fatherless. Many can remind us that just because there's a body in your house, it doesn't guarantee it to be a mentor or role model. What I've learned along the way is that there are a number of people I call cheerleaders stationed there to help us through the mud holes of life. Sir Walter Raleigh reportedly threw down his cloak over a mud puddle so that Queen Elizabeth wouldn't get her feet muddy. Fact or fiction, the imagery is apropos.

We've often seen the hero in a movie say, "We can do this the easy way or the hard way." A lot of people are hard headed and bound and determined to learn things the hard way. For those who are willing to listen and be alert, there's an army of people out there waiting to fill in the gaps in our lives when our loved ones can't be everywhere at once. We've all heard that we have entertained angels unaware. Someone at different times has been directed to help us. They may have helped spare us from a bad experience or given us that boost we needed to crawl out of the hole.

We know we cannot go through life by ourselves. We don't have to. We're promised aid from our Maker. Maybe it's time to open our eyes to what is in front of them.

Snob

I am not a snob; sometimes my wife may look at my work attire at the end of the day and think maybe slob, but I can't say as I give a rip. I am what I am. Jeff Jordan, chicken grower, from over at Pine Forest once told my wife I was his kind of guy when we returned to our house years ago from a double date and he caught me messing with my toe nails. I must have been wearing sandals. He claims it had something to do with a coat hanger. I must have gotten the idea from Everybody Loves Raymond. I don't think I'm that smart on my own.

I recently read that it did matter where you live. The author talked about the influence others have on you. It goes beyond being judged by the company you keep. I think it may kinda lean over toward the concept of dressing for success. It's hard to look too snotty in an 80 El Camino. I don't think I consciously strived to live a certain place in town. I actually bought a farm once to build my wife a new house; after months of clearing land and tearing down an old house, she drove out one day, saw a bunch of coyote skins hanging on nearby fence posts, and put the kabash on that plan!

My next plan was to move away from a deteriorating neighborhood and find a deal like Chip and Joanna from Waco do. They always picked older houses in good neighborhoods and updated them. We did that until the female in an all male house said it was time to build that dream house before the boys went to college. This time we had the chance to build the first house in the back of a new section of an established neighborhood. We did. Three years later I find she doesn't like the one and only two story we ever had. Luckily, I got out of that one and moved around the corner. I didn't have to build again; Mama was ok.

What part if anything did it matter where we lived? For most of their lives the boys grew up in safe neighborhoods where we never worried about crime. Most of the people around were working folks doing ok; a fair number were professionals and business owners. Most of the kids' friends did well in school and aimed for college or came back home at some time for the family business. It did seem like the ones from the hood who came over did have big goals and plans for graduate schools or dental or medical schools. Like I said, I'm not a snob. I had no big plan to live in a particular place.

I don't think it hurt the kids to grow up in a good neighborhood where most people had higher expectations for their kids. It guaranteed nothing; it did not make you better than anyone, but I think that if any of my hard work and sacrifice helped give my kids a vision of a better life, then I am glad we went through the gyrations of moving and building over the years. You can't get too uppity or smarty in a small town. You are who you are and people accept you for it. The only thing I know is that I am no better than anyone else. Things mean nothing to me. What matters is if anything I did including providing a good safe place for my kids to grow up in, helped them get off to a good start, as a lot of you have done for your kids, then I'm glad. What I do know, however, is that if Mama and I didn't teach them some values and what's important along the way, what you live in matters squat. I have to say in all matters of raising kids is thank you Lord for what you gave us and how you blessed. I hope I haven't squandered what you loaned me for a short spell.

My Prescription

My former coworker and friend Becky Berry got me in to see her pulmonologist Dr. Mac in Paris a few years back for breathing issues. While doing a routine follow up exam later he had me tilt my head back. That's when he saw it. The tumors were located on the edge of his expertise, and a young fellow throat surgeon said they were at the edge of his specialty. They collaborated, unwrapped the tumors from my vocal cords removed some of my thyroid, saved my voice, maybe even my life. Dr. Erickson hadn't wanted to alarm me before the surgery; afterwards he told my wife we had a blessing. He told me he wasn't fibbing about my prognosis; he just didn't think 5% sounded very good. No chemo or radiation was needed. I, or should I say my wife, keeps a close eye on my neck and throat. I think it's just an excuse for her to see if I'm washing my neck like I should.

As the bumper sticker predicted, things happen. I heard what makes God laugh is people making plans. Back at work my coworkers were encouraging; one rather graphic description by a less than sensitive employee told me how my head was just kinda hanging off as they did their thing. That will stick with you. With friends like that, who needs the others.

What about that old nagging feeling you get when one lymph nodes swell or a neck muscle gets sore. Your mind can play the dickens with your imagination. You don't get a medal for stupidity, but you can't spend your free time thinking the worst either. I try to be observant and occasionally let em check me. The good thing about getting older is that they can sometimes hide your scars among your wrinkles, just like a good pair of glasses can hide those bags under your eyes. A doctor told me he could improve my vision which had deteriorated from my Air Force days. He said I would still need reading glasses. Why not wear what you need instead of having to carry them around and lose them. I passed. This way I can still hide my bags; instead of looking 100, I only look 90. Who said men are vain.

I share these thoughts with you because we've all fought and still fight the good fight. Sometimes my wife says she just has to have a good cry. Me, I think I just have to go get me a good burger or hamburger steak with grilled onions and brown gravy at South Main Café in Paris. My friend Larry Finney and I used to spend the last week each school year making the rounds of Cooper, Cumby, Brashear, Como, The Bluff, Roxton, and any other place that had a good café. That went a long way toward shaking off the coils of our mortal souls after a long year's journey of stomping out ignorance as my grandpa used to say. Whatever works, do it. Life will pile poop on your head. You don't have to stand there and let it accumulate. Go find you a good café and leave your cares behind you.

Bofe

I haven't met many retired people who are unhappy, especially if they are able to make ends meet satisfactorily. Most of us wouldn't mind a little extra loot, if only to help others out. The question now as it has always been in your life is what would you trade for the extra resources? When it comes down to it most of us have accepted our circumstances and don't feel a particular urgency to shake things up. I've kept enough side work to keep me as busy as I want. My wife considered part-time work, but didn't want to give up her flexibility as a substitute teacher in her old school in her favorite grade because it might limit her opportunity to babysit Emmie and her future siblings when Emmie's mommy needed her.

The key ingredient in the schedule of us retired guys is that word flexibility. A number of us have kept or taken something part-time to give us a little mad money. We know there won't likely be any cost of living increases in our retirement checks, so a little bit of work helps while we still can. It is almost intoxicating to wake up and realize no more e-mails to check every 5 seconds and no ties to tie. How could I give this up after 42 years in the same profession? I still love to work; now I just work for me. I get to pick when and where I want to work.

With the freedom of retirement comes a whole new set of good problems. A friend had taught 57 years in a rural school, had the school building named after her, and still came to work. When asked why she did it, she said if she stayed home she would end up being a full-time chauffeur for everyone.

We all need something to make us get up each morning and to look forward to. For some it may be a wet kiss from four legs that want out or want us to go for a walk. It may be the only kiss you'll get that day, so don't knock it. I frequently remind you that inactivity is the big bugaboo to avoid as we age. Like my lawn equipment and the old man's tractor, the longer you let em sit idle, the harder they are to start. Our bodies and minds are machines that have to be used to keep down the rust.

Like vitamins and probiotics, a daily dose may be required. A friend of mine with occasional high blood pressure swears by his 30 minute walks as a means of quickly dropping his numbers. Exercise of any kind increases the release of endorphins that make us feel good, so does looking at videos on your phone of the grandbaby. Instead of choosing between the two, make like Cuba Gooding Jr. in the movie Radio. When asked to pick from two desserts offered by Coach Ed Harris, he promptly gave my favorite and logical answer, "Bofe."

Speaking of Pain

As the aging process sets in, our computer in the brain begins a search sometimes to remind us of where the pain likely started. Most football players can figure out why the knee hurts; quarterbacks begin to think of blows to the head and how it might relate to memory issues. Someone waved smelling salts under their noses and said, "Get back in there." Some girls are beginning to learn about headers in soccer and possible head or neck issues.

As morning arrives we begin sorting out the pain issues. Is it a temporary one or is it permanent? If you are an optimist, you hope that it, like many other pains, that like a stray cat or a dropped-off dog, it was just passing through. Like the cat and dog, we can mentally feed it and now have a pet; we can refuse to feed it mentally, and hopefully it will go inhabit someone else.

Then there is the come-and-go guy, like unpredictable family members, who show up, stay a little while, and then are gone. Sometimes a short visit lingers on. Some pains are like that. They start off with Equate and end up requiring Tylenol 3 or worse.

Another pain comes with no doubt of its intention. It hurts from day 1. Sometimes high heel shoes can be the culprit. I've watched my wife try every kind of shoe she could find, but nothing seems to permanently fix the pain in the foot that has moved to a new category—pain in the butt.

You may consider surgery, but many others, particularly those with aching backs who had that surgery, have often found it only makes it worse. It almost becomes a crap shoot. I've known people have screws put into the back and then taken out. Your weight is all on your feet. When you get desperate due to the pain and have surgery, you pray it doesn't end up worse.

A friend of mine has worn out three recliners sleeping in one since he was rear ended years ago. Some people have spent a small fortune on special beds and pillows from Minnesota. Who dares to add up all the loot spent on TV ads that promised to ease our pain.

One area I hesitate to approach is because I might be guilty. It has to be a fact that our weight could be a factor. I try to find skinny guys and girls with health problems and point out to my wife that watching your weight might not be all it's cracked up to be. Yet, deep down I know shedding a few pounds could ease wear and tear on my knees, feet, heart, etc., maybe reducing the need for pain relievers or having painful surgery. I think my wife and I know all that. We actually both have been trying harder and lost weight.

Still, sugar cookies whisper I love you's to my wife as she walks by them in the grocery store. Real Coke bubbles and fizzes at me in the convenience store and tells me how it misses me and promises to no longer affect my blood sugar. You dastardly villains know how to hurt a guy. We're slightly encouraged as our pants get droopy and a new hole is added to the belt.

In the past we have had some good exercise equipment go to Goodwill for tax deductions. Before that they made great clothes racks. Early on one of those bikes seemed to get aggravated when I kept spilling my milkshake on my sweat pants as I bounced my knees up and down.

I had been taking sugar meds for years as punishment for substituting Coke for water as we mowed yards. Finally my wife and I have a common enemy now as she, too, is now motivated to eat better in hope of being around a little longer for a few more of those jelly jar sticky kisses from grandkids.

Looking like Tar Baby from fingertip to elbow and wearing jelly camouflage, Emmie makes it tough to sneak in and steal a jelly-flavored kiss. Someday she's gonna learn how to eat with utensils instead of her fingers. Until then, we're just gonna have to suck it up and carry some Wet Wipes if we want to get some of that sugar that doesn't jack up the old A1C.

Priorities

I'm sitting on the bed crying, completely destroyed by my mother's simple response, "No, you're not." When asked why,she simply said, " You told me, you didn't ask me." Did I tell you she was tough.   A woman abandoned with 5 kids doesn't have much room for indecision. Maybe I had gotten a little cocky. I was the new student body president-elect and had a date with one of the prettiest girls in high school. It had absolutely nothing to do with her hourglass figure. I was not impressed that she was the first girl I had gone with who could wear a strapless dress.

It was simply her sweet personality; it had nothing to do with half the boys in school turning a slight shade of green. The double date with Tommy and Linda to introduce her to me had been great. Now the bottom dropped out. Needless to say it didn't take her long to find a guy who didn't have to share the 57 Chevy or maybe even get permission to drive it. Lesson learned. The next time I saw her she was out of school and bringing her future husband some supper to Farmers Co-op as we worked late unloading boxcars.

She still wasn't ugly, and I still didn't own a car as I poor-boyed it through Texas Tech. I still shared the family car at home and caught rides helping pay drivers with gas money back and forth to Lubbock while I was in college. Keep the main thing the main thing. Where do my boys get that self-discipline? You can do about anything you set your mind to. Yes, also learn the difference between necessities and luxuries or "want to's" and "have to's."

Earlier it had been true love for a whole week in junior high. This one's dad was our Texaco man. She was Church of Christ and I was Baptist, but I knew we could make it work. She and I exchanged necklaces we'd gotten at the State Fair. The hearts were engraved. This was the real thing, or so I thought. Then trouble reared its ugly head. I told her I would go to a skating party with her. A fine excuse to hold a woman's hand all night. You guessed it. I proudly announced to mama and the girls that I had a date to go skating. The dark cloud loomed overhead as she quizzed me about the time of the soiree. A frown crossed her face, her jaws twitched, and that malevolent, accusatory finger touched a specific baseball practice schedule on the Frigidaire.

"You can, but you can hang up your ball glove." End of discussion. Love had clouded my judgment. How could fate have been so cruel. What to do, what to do? Actually, after the initial shock wore off, I knew there was no choice. I had given my heart and soul to the baseball diamond at an early age. Heck, my first year of organized baseball after the farm was predicated on my playing for a coach who would buy an insurance policy from my dad. That gives a whole new meaning to bonus baby. I think I moved to town after the baseball draft was over.

I'm not saying that baseball was almost like a religion in my house, but it was close. Mom rooted for the haughty Yankees, while I idolized Stan Musial and the St. Louis Cardinals. I'm not saying that baseball was important to me; however, it is true that when my first Little League game was rained out, I fell on my bed and cried like a baby. I guess the die was cast. I had found my first love. Well, at least until I got a whiff later of "I'll

25

never forget old what's her name's" perfume. Then I had to stop and do some serious thinking about priorities!

Darkness

On a recent visit to a shut-in from church a really strong Christian and lifelong Sunday school teacher for over 50 years made a depressing comment. She had broken her leg and was sitting in her wheelchair at home. The house was silent. She said all she had to do was to sit there staring at four walls. I remember Jim Reeves singing, "Four walls to hear me, four walls to see, four walls too near me, closing in on me." I had just left another lady who was fairly restricted by her long not-so-portable oxygen line that I tried not to trip over in her dimly lit room. She chose to leave the blinds pulled which fit the mood.

People actively involved in their senior years often get sidelined by physical ailments and then have to fight the mental battle. You can call it blues, mild depression, sadness, or feeling down; it amounts to about the same. People left alone without much human contact can find it hard to keep a stiff upper lip. When you're temporarily or permanently sidelined, it's hard to no longer feel useful or important. You can come to feel like a burden on others. We usually cook for or eat a daily meal with my father-in-law. He is still active, but recent death of his spouse has not helped his MS. He referred to the meals as a burden on us. I think we feel like we are just trying to help him make it through that hard time of bereavement. He's making progress, but the blues drop in from time to time.

As families and friends sometimes we get too busy and overlook these guys. We're all swamped. Retirement is often busier than our working years. Us old retirees wouldn't trade the flexibility we now have and not having to constantly check

E-mails. Still, it seems we have to budget our time to get around to everything. One fall, one slip, and we're over on the other side looking at four walls closing in on us. Scripture says, "I must work the works of him that sent me, while it is day: the night cometh, when no man can work."

With age hopefully comes wisdom. We hope we've learned what's important, the earlier the better. Our elderly friends are reminding us of the night coming. We can focus on our prayer life and Bible study when our bodies no longer cooperate. We can dial that phone to spread a little cheer until old Arthur makes the finger too stiff to dial. An old friend recently passed in a nursing home. She had a list of people on speed dial as she lay there in bed. She'd say, "Whatcha doing?" I'm hoping I'll still have her drive to fight off the darkness when the night settles in on me.

Made In The Shade

August temperatures slipped into July during the summer of 2018. Electric use was at an all-time high. Those working outdoors were placing a premium on finding shade. Dairy herds bunched up under the shelter of oak trees as a respite from the heat. These conditions brought back memories of older fellas voicing approval or envy of whatever my situation was by telling me, "Boy, you got it made in the shade."

In a lot of ways that introduction of air conditioning, especially in the South and West, revolutionized living and working there. It didn't do a lot for the animals in the fields and pastures, but it may have improved things for those who got the benefit of AC being added to homes and some work situations.

Having grown up on a farm I totally understand the value of shade. Without access to AC back then, shade meant everything. People often built their homes around trees or planted trees to help provide some protection from the sun. Even some occupations or skills like shade tree mechanic told you the importance of trees in the scheme of things. For the most part today the ordinary person in the city isn't likely to give much thought to such things as protection from the sun. They simply lower the thermostat.

Even God realized the importance of shade as He provided a cloud by day to protect His people as they fled Egypt and slavery. Having it made in the shade is an interesting concept. Knowing how valuable and even life saving the presence of shade can or could be to those humans and animals destined to spend their days in the sun, shade comes to symbolize much more than merely being sheltered by a tree. Shade might represent comfort or a better quality of life than someone could have without the benefit of nature's protection.

In the past, people did not take shade for granted. I remember how much I looked forward to stacking up peanut vines around a post in the field to let the green goobers dry. What a thrill it was to get to sit in the shade of this newly created shock of peanut vines with tar paper on top of the stack for the peanuts' protection. The little shade it produced in the cool, damp East Texas sand was just right for a little boy with sand cracks between his toes, incurred while working barefoot in the hot Texas sand.

Whenever I've heard that expression of having it made in the shade, it immediately takes me back to a simpler time, a slower time, when things like shade or peanut shocks or neighbors helping each other were valued and not taken for granted.

It Ain't You Babe

Back in the 60's The Turtles had a hit with Bob Dylan's song, "It Ain't Me Babe." People need to be accountable for their messages, but they also need to do something else. I have run into a jillion people who are compassionate, caring, giving people and generally very sensitive. They have one glaring Achilles heel; they think life is about them. It's not. When wrongs come their way and light on their doorstep, they put it all on their back and totally embrace the whole shebang. They shouldn't.

All of us are looking at life through tinted glasses as we have things happen to us and have to grapple with what it has done to our lives. People who tend to be some of the most caring people go into overdrive as they struggle to figure out why someone would do so and so to them. What did they do wrong? Nothing.

People who are more pragmatic, realistic, and have a better handle on how life works tend to avoid a lot of the anguish and soul searching that some of those who place an inordinate value on wanting everyone to like us and value us. What a lot of some of the nicest people in the world don't understand is, it ain't you, babe. Some people who actually may look like shy introverts actually have the same ego issue that some of those cocky showoffs do that are always trying to get our attention.

What many people do not grasp and waste a lot of emotional energy and tears and carry some heavy reservoirs of resentment toward other persons or organizations is that it ain't personal. They aren't thinking about you at all. You have to understand agendas. If you get in the way of a supervisor's or a company's agenda, you're about to step in dodo. It is not personal. You're not that important. So what that you came early, stayed late, spent your own money to accomplish a goal. It all comes down to the agendas of others.

The older you are in an organization the more pressure you are likely to feel to head on down the road. Younger managers may begin to tack on extra duties, freeze pay raises, or make unreasonable training demands to get you to start thinking of retirement. The company's goal may be to replace older with younger and cheaper or more technologically skilled young people. There's a constant ying and yang between old and young in many organizations. The older have the wisdom, experience, and higher salaries.

The younger think they have the wisdom, which they don't, and they want those higher salaries. Youzz in the way. Nothing personal. Don't let it hit you in the behind as you leave. You thought you were valued and honored. That was yesterday. Get your ego out of the way. Do not take those feelings of anger and disappointment with you. Leave them. I guarantee there are no tears or time being wasted on you.

This is not a bitter response. This is a plea to that group of people who may have been coaxed or shoved or dragged into moving on and into retirement. Get rid of those garbage feelings. No one is back in the office grieving or wasting time thinking about you. Look, we served our time and gave them our best.

Now it's time to move on and find joy, fulfillment, and contentment in a new phase in your life. Let go of grudges and bad feelings toward people or organizations that haven't lost a minute's sleep over your departure. Remember, the greatest revenge is success. When you run into the old guys, give em your biggest smile and mean it. It will drive them crazy.

24 Hours

He removed his glasses and raised his eyes. "I'm sorry but you have 24 hours to live. Get your affairs in order and say your goodbyes."

Tim McGraw's song "Live Like You Were Dying" asks what you'd do if you knew you only had a set amount of time left. Job reads, "The length of our lives is decided beforehand—the number of months we will live. You have settled it and it can't be changed." Days of our Lives started each show with the sand falling through the hourglass as the narrator says, "Like sand through the hourglass, so are the days of our lives." The clock begins ticking the minute we're born. Our life is measured down to the final breath. Ephesians tells us to "Redeem the time."

If you could look into the future as Scrooge did in the movie The Christmas Carol and see your death, would it make you a new person? With 24 hours left in your life, what would you do differently? Tim sang about skydiving and riding bulls. How about you? How would you compress your bucket list like Jack Nicholson and Morgan Freeman in Bucket List. Would it be something exciting or would it be something with more significant meaning?

From time to time we get warnings of meteors coming into our atmosphere. Some are large enough to take out you and me. Does it give us pause for a moment to do some self-examination? A man I knew had a blood clot pass through his heart with a 2% survival rate. I asked him if he looked at life differently. He said he figured it wasn't his time yet. Staring at the grill of the truck that had come into my lane, I read the letters on the license plate in what I believed was my last thought. Opening my eyes I saw the oncoming vehicle was now behind me in my rear view mirror. It wasn't my time.

Given a time check worth 24 hours, would you dive with the sharks or forgive a family member? Would you choose to drive a pace car at Indy 500 or contact a child who has not spoken to you in ten years? Do you bungee jump off the Golden Gate Bridge or track down an old friend or ex you hurt? Would you buy a new Lexus or visit your priest and make your confessions?

Compared to eternity our life is shorter than a twinkle in God's eye. What has it accomplished? Matthew tells us to "Lay not up for yourselves treasures upon earth, where moth and rust does corrupt, and where thieves break through and steal." With 24 hours or 24 years, what could we accomplish for eternity if we determined to make every second count until the trumpet sounded its last call.

Veteran's Day

It was Veteran's Day weekend ahead as I left the neighborhood. Old Glory attached to metal flagpoles placed there by Boy Scouts lined both sides of each street. For the moment, the cynical, jaded world, ignorant of the sacrifices made to be able to have our flag and fly it freely, hadn't been successful in destroying one of the last vestiges of freedom not diluted or removed.

The drive through the country to the rural school helped let the cares slide off as I took a deep sigh. Memories of the many months of campaigning for my son for Judge came flooding back as I remembered every rural driveway and fence where I had helped place signs. It also brought a warm feeling knowing the thousands of miles and tanks of gas for my old truck, the high flood waters and muddy roads and new auto body squeals, lost hubcaps and tons of mud underneath the truck frame all helped contribute to a winning race and many new friendships.

Pulling into the country schoolyard the line of flags surrounding the cemetery across from the school helped me focus on my imminent speech honoring veterans in the school gymnasium. Among them were vets from several wars. A couple were now deputy sheriffs pulling double duty today to serve their fellow citizens. The ag boys and girls escorted us to our seats on the gym floor. The beautiful gym and the group of local parents reminded me of my rural upbringing and the feeling that comes from the closeness of a small community.

The students did an excellent job of honoring us with homemade cards and flags. Their patriotic songs and poems warmed our hearts. In a sea of indifferent feelings, we were showered with a warm cloud of appreciation.

It was a blessed opportunity to help honor the visiting veterans who had sacrificed so much. I got to remind everyone of the true value of service. Serve others and you will be happy; serve yourself and you will not. We remembered the shrinking numbers of vets from WWII, Korea, and Vietnam and the more recent sacrifices of veterans from Afghanistan, Syria, and Iraq. We reminded the students of ultimate sacrifices we honored on Memorial Day each May.

We know that there may never be an end to the continual need to honor those who continue to serve in future conflicts. Others will make the ultimate sacrifice for their fellow man as the threats to our freedom will continue to require our sons and daughters to be willing to give all.

It Is What You Make It

It was off-season football conditioning and distance running. I was leading the pack to the chagrin of some less motivated runners. I couldn't help it. I loved running and as Forest Gump said, "I was just runding and runding." The head coach called me over to congratulate me on winning a really spirited election for student body president for the next year and to add how proud he was to have a football player win the honor. Truthfully, the other 3 guys would have made great presidents. They represented the football, basketball, and tennis teams. The 4 of us were the male members of the National Honor Society. It doesn't get much more balanced or fun than that.

Setting priorities is tough. I didn't have the nerve to tell Coach I wouldn't be playing next year. I had to have the money from working at the drive-in theater on the weekends to help pay for my college. We didn't know a lot about it, and there was very little financial aid back then. It was called working your way through school. I played baseball every summer, but I always had to work during the school year at the drive-in and Farmers Co-op in the spring. My senior year they let me work around baseball and keep my jobs. I'll always be thankful for people like that helping me out. People line up to help you when you're trying to do a good job.

Those next four years were some variations of a similar schedule. At Tech it was waiting on tables at the Student Union, catering banquets, and working the circulation desk at the Tech library while opening and closing it on weekends. I eventually got a few dollars from Air Force ROTC and got free room and board my last year by being a resident advisor in the dorm after I had served as dorm president my junior year.

The summers were Farmers Co-op, Hi-Vue Drive In, mowing yards, doodle bugging for oil in Louisiana swamps, doing construction and being trained as an Air Force officer for upcoming leadership jobs. We had 700 in ROTC at Tech as we prepared for Vietnam. I got to serve as one of 2 commanders my senior year. What a thrill to lead the troops through the middle of the campus.

I've said all this to tell anyone that they can do whatever they want in America. One good parent, my mom, sent me $5.00 every other month. I got $5.00 every other month for giving blood at the blood bank. You really can eat an elephant one bite at a time. Put your head down, drag that sack, and don't stop till you get to the end of the row. Life is a cotton pickin good time.

Crossing Jordan

Stopped by Burgers and Fries for my Sunday special. They started fixing it when I hit the door. It was almost ready before I could get my drink and find my seat. Small town service. Love it. As I was chowing down on my burger one of my followers of my weekly post stopped by to tell me her mom and her best friend were heading to the Holy Land to be baptized in the Jordan River.

Great memories came flooding back of my time in the Middle East and in particular, Israel. I ended up at their table where we had a rollicking good time talking about the upcoming trip. One lady was a child of 70 while her buddy was a tad older, hoping to fulfill a lifelong dream visit to Jesus' old stomping grounds.

I was jealous of their upcoming adventure. The older lady was apprehensive about an upcoming back surgery to be performed when she returned from her trip, but her concern was topped by her excitement of visiting the Wailing Wall and following Christ's example of being baptized by John the Baptist as he immersed the Savior in that clear, cold Jordan. I still remember the awe I felt knowing this was the very same waters that I got to stand in. Just as I had as I walked along the shores of Lake Gennesaret or Sea of Galilee, I couldn't get over the fact that I, too, was in the same physical geographical area where the Savior had walked and lived for his short 33 years.

Coming from Texas over the years, I've had to adjust my perception of space and size. I remember how close the states seemed together in New England. I had similar feelings as I went from country to country in Europe and the Middle East.

The Holy Land was long and skinny. It was hard to imagine that this was literally the focal point of so many countries. Everything was so compact, yet God chose to make this the center of his universe. Shrines and memorials cover everything. Put all tourism aside, they cannot move and have not moved the Jordan River, Dead Sea, Jerusalem, Nazareth and on it goes.

I didn't need to spend time in the Middle East to be a believer. What did happen was getting this permanent feeling of how real it all was and is. Despite facing male and female soldiers armed with automatic weapons wherever I went, I still had this kind of strong desire or yearning to stay there or maybe live there. As you walk around, you have a sense of danger and slight dread. Yet you can't help having a feeling of excitement knowing where you are and how real the land has become to you when you finally see it with your own eyes.

I'm grateful I didn't have to feel the scars as doubting Thomas did after his Savior's resurrection to be a believer. Stilll, what a thrill and honor to know you got to see the same shores and wade those cold waters of the Jordan River, all the while knowing I won't have to cross it by myself. No, never alone.

Then and Now

This may be more of a guy thing, but I seem to remember Glen Campbell's song, "Dreams of the Everyday Housewife" where she thinks back about the gown she wore in high school that made the boys swallow their Juicy Fruit gum. I just added the last part. There's nothing wrong with thinking back on the past and hopefully smiling. The problem lies in constantly going back, almost living there. We've all known some jock or beauty queen who has a tendency to steer conversations back to their glory days. You often wonder if they may have selective memory.

Living in the past means we don't have to do as much living in the present. A lot of this may stem from dissatisfaction with how life has turned out for the person. Some people turn to alcohol or drugs, while others forego reality and focus on nostalgia. The topic of class reunions comes up as old boyfriends and girlfriends may reconnect there and try to rekindle the old flame, sometimes going home to continue the newly revived relationship by electronic media. Sometime feel good stories come out of this; sometimes troubled marriages have trouble handling the strain of an extra presence in the marriage. Most likely problems existed before, but became more apparent after the nostalgic trip.

Another song by Garth Brooks, "Thank God for Unanswered Prayers," gives a more realistic look at what might have been but thankfully didn't happen. Dan Folgerburg's song, "Old Lang Syne," is another story of gratitude for a relationship that stayed in the past. Nostalgia gave way to reality.

When my friends start in on the good old days I always start wondering how I approach this. A marriage can survive a little nostalgia but probably not handle much love searching on the Internet. Most wives take a dim view of things like that. Infidelity, physically or only emotionally, still has a way of chipping away at the foundation of trust in each other.

Part of the solution to living in the past is to create new experiences and memories in the present. Good old days make us smile because we selectively forget the bad memories or embellish our actions from the past. Creating new positive experiences gives us something to occupy our minds and improve how we feel about ourselves.

Happy Days struck a chord in the 70's and 80's as it brought back the relatively peaceful years of late 50's and early 60's. Some people say they can't find a thing to watch on TV, or they keep it tuned to stations like TV Land and Hallmark, and Inspirational Network. A lot of us long for simpler times. We just have to fight the good fight of the present and not let living in the past overshadow the joy of real life.

Love People, Use Things

Things are only valuable to us if they are useful. Relationships with people are what are most valuable and fulfilling in our lives. Simply by looking at older people and determining what they have valued in their lives and what outlook they have toward life in their later years we are able to determine what matters most in their lives. Things are not able to teach us lessons about life.

Love is action. The lives of Mother Theresa and Albert Schweitzer are the epitome of someone willing to give all to love people. Missionary Jim Elliot and friends died while risking their lives to show love to the Huaorani tribesmen of Ecuador.

Most of us won't be called on to travel across the world to help total strangers, but we should be willing to give up things if it is necessary for us to care for the person across the street.

It is only when we interact with people that we come to understand how much more valuable people are than things. It is important to understand that things are what we use in our daily lives and that they are not as important as relationships with people.

We say we love people when we value them more than we are interested in using them for our own purposes. It is okay to give value to material goods as long as we do not place more value on them than on people and our relationships with them.

We cannot have a life full of purpose and meaning if we do not realize how much more valuable relationships with people are than owning things.

Many people feel that if they could get a little more money then all would be great. Studies tell us that a most recent survey found that happiness can be increased for most people if they can get at least $70,000 a year in income.

In addition, it was found that over $70,000 a year did not increase their happiness that much. Research tells us that half of all lottery winners end up in financial trouble.

Numerous winners have suffered great tragedies due to issues related to acquiring instant wealth. Money is not the issue; the problem is allowing it to change our values and letting things take a wrong priority over human relationships.

Things have no feelings or emotions and therefore cannot create lasting feelings within us. On the other hand, it is the emotional connections from relationships that we come to value most if we can truly understand what is most valuable in life.

Relationships with people are the most valuable things that we possess because they are also the longest lasting. They are so fulfilling because they fill our lives with lasting feelings and emotions. Relationships are valuable because they have eternal values.

Good relationships create lasting feelings as we become involved in other people's lives. They help us make emotional connections that things are not able to create. Relationships create those strong ties and feelings.

They have the ability to grow stronger and deeper as long as we live. Material things only last for a season, but strong relationships last a lifetime. Our attachment to things may not grow, whereas our feelings for other people may become deeper and stronger. This reinforces the idea to love people and use things.

The Greatest Revenge

I know that "vengeance is mine sayeth the Lord." Still, there is something really satisfying about seeing the worm turn. One company has had numerous chief executives, some not lasting very long. A friend of mine suffered the same fate but started his own business and is very successful today.

Often, relationships hinge on how much potential a spouse might have. I've known of numerous relationships discouraged by ambitious parents because they didn't think the prospective in-law would be a good provider for their child. Many families lived to regret their actions as the prospect became successful.

One really satisfying scenario involves a spouse dumping a partner for some new partner based on looks or potential gain.

How sweet it is when the jilted partner overcomes the breakup and goes on to work hard and eventually be a successful person who gets the last laugh. It's especially satisfying when the runaway spouse crashes and burns or suffers a similar fate that the first spouse had to endure. How do you like me now?

In relationships it is easy for one spouse to be dominant and totally control a person's life. This may degenerate over time to verbal abuse and constantly putting the person down, implying they will never "amount to anything." Long periods of brain washing can scar a person for life and cause them to believe it to be true. How great it is to see a person crawl out of the pit of despair and reach a lifelong goal in spite of years of constant abuse.

A final element of complete revenge comes when we have to forgive that person and refuse to give them any power over our lives and not let them take our joy. We can obsess over past slights when the slighter hardly knows we exist and certainly isn't losing any sleep thinking about us.

When you're able to look the tormentor in the eye, smile, and thank them for helping you become the strong person you are today, then you have succeeded. They no longer have any control over you or your joy. Next time you see them in the store don't go to the next aisle. Just smile at them. It messes with their mind.

Pursuit of Happiness

The Declaration of Independence guarantees us the right of pursuit of happiness. In a movie of the same name Will Smith shows us the high cost of making that right a reality. There are a thousand platitudes about nothing worth having is easy. Today, a lot of people have come to believe that the right to pursue happiness should be accompanied by the guarantee of finding happiness.

Like most parents, we did all we could to give our children the opportunity to pursue their interest in sports, music, or anything else they showed interest in. I've always told parents to do everything they could to follow up on any interest a child demonstrated. Taking the approach of the auto mechanic, "pay me now or pay me later," my advice to parents was that anything you do for a child is cheaper than jail later.

A friend of mine was paralyzed in an auto crash. Another friend got him to use power tools from his wheel chair as he did beautiful finishing work on wood. He told me his accident was the best thing that ever happened to him. He was able to steer away from trouble and focus on his pursuit of happiness.

We helped put our sons into a position where they could pursue their dreams. They had no guarantees but knew we would support what they pursued. Along the way they had to help me mow a few thousand yards to help make their dreams a reality. Today they are both successful in their fields of endeavor.

Their mother stayed home when the boys were little, returning to school in her 30's. We did all we could to help her realize her dream of becoming an elementary school teacher. We sacrificed a lot to help her succeed. We supported her any way we could. Today she continues to thank us for helping her in her pursuit of happiness.

For me it was seeing my father abandon us five kids leaving a forty plus year old housewife with little formal education to learn to sew blue jeans to feed us. I mowed yards, sold greeting cards, and any other chore to pay for my school lunches.

Years later in college with no money, no car, and one hand-me-down suit my father left behind, I was able to graduate from college as a second lieutenant in the Air Force and teach college English while working on my Masters.

While I was in college my mom would send me five dollars every couple of months with an apology for not doing more. I told her that her support was worth far more than any money. Every other month I got five dollars at the blood bank plus some free Fresca and cookies from some non-ugly girls.

If you want it bad enough you can do it. I love this land where I'm free to try, win or lose. That's all I ask. No guarantees.

Choices Do Make a Difference

I was filling in for the pastor last Sunday night. Looking over at the youth group on my left I told them choices do make a difference. One wrong decision can almost sidetrack a dream; that is unless you get the talk from Mom in the 57 Chevy which goes like this, "If you get a girl pregnant, we'll raise the child if we need to, but you're going to college." Case closed. That was the kind of advice that will get your attention. I was probably busy thinking about my baseball game that night.

If you're determined enough you can overcome almost anything. Fortunately for many of us we made the choices that didn't hold us back or make it really hard to follow our dreams. It helps to constantly remind yourself along the way what your goals are.

Becoming a parent as a teenager or piling up debt in college can really slow down achieving your goals. Young couples copying mom and dad desiring new and big things unaware or ignoring how long it took parents to get there can almost bury themselves in debt. Young marriages can crumble under the weight of all that pressure.

My son and his wife have taught it in church and practiced the Dave Ramsey program of limiting debt and paying cash when they can. I've learned some good things from them about financial choices. It is a tough uphill fight to limit charging in the face of promotions and pressure to get it all now. One stumped toe, one medical emergency, can send the house of cards falling down.

Day-to-day living is tough enough.

Just getting by is almost a victory in itself. Now let's throw in some really dumb choices like infidelity or other totally avoidable activities tied to selfishness. Not considering what you're giving up hurts everyone. I value too much what I've been blessed with to throw it away. Looking back many people belatedly recognize what a terrible price they've paid in giving up what years of hard work have helped them put together.

There are a zillion broken homes with broken hearts to match. I was glad when my parents divorced. We were instantly poor but at least it was peaceful again and I felt more secure. I also vowed not to make the same bad choices my dad did. I think about all those great times he missed with us kids and the grandkids.

My childhood experience has helped me to be doubly determined to be a man of character who knows what is important. I love the security of coming home to a warm house and people who love me. I pray I never make choices that jeopardize all that really matters in my life.

Fight the Good Fight

Regarding old age a friend jokingly told me if you want a big funeral, die young. The crowd gets thinner when you're outliving your peers. Sometimes I feel 30, but it quickly goes away once I bend to retrieve something from the floor. We've heard the phrase, "Help, I've fallen and I can't get up."

I don't fall; I just like sitting in the floor or on the grass! That way I can sort laundry or pull weeds sitting down. I just need something to pull on when I start to get up. A leaf blower is an excellent staff when you point it at the ground.

If you don't laugh, you will cry. My friend Finis was 97 and told me, "If you can't bite 'em, gum' em." Life is about picking your battles. Epictetus said, "It's not what happens to you, but how you react to it that matters." The bumper sticker reminds you "_____happens."

What do you want to accomplish around the dash on your headstone? Dylan Thomas said, "Do not go gentle into that dark night." Released from prison and contemplating suicide in a movie about prison life, Morgan Freeman chooses life; he said it was "time to get busy living or get busy dying." He made the right choice.

In our later years it's easy to act frustrated trying to open jar lids and reading small print. One song I heard growing up went, "I used to jump just like a deer, and now I need a new landing gear." The challenge is to accept what you can't do and celebrate what you can. We tell shut-ins in my church to be prayer warriors. They also keep phone lines hot checking on each other and letting me know who needs assistance.

Roger Miller had a song about old friends arm and arm stepping up onto a curb. The older we become, we may struggle to get up from being seated. If you and your friend are equally challenged, the trick is who is helping whom. Whoever makes it up first is the winner and number one assistant. Somewhere in there should be a good laugh.

Hanging out with friends you have to pool your efforts. The one who hears best has to translate and relay messages. The one who can see has to stay observant and help avoid falls and the dreaded broken hip. A friend was almost 90 and still driving a car. He was probably legally blind.

Rather than give in to his disability, he continued to drive while his wife served as his eyes as she told him where to turn. They eventually hired a driver for weekly trips to the grocery store. Giving up your independence is a tough pill to swallow.

Stay home as long as you can. Get help for your spouse before it physically breaks you. Take consolation in the fact that you're not in the boat alone.

Springtime and Freedom

It feels like a time of renewal. The bulbs I dug up in the pasture last fall are starting to bloom in the beds. They looked like lilies and reminded me of Good Friday and the crucifixion and then Easter and the resurrection. It's a time for thankfulness for His sacrifice.

Sunday evening comes the Easter egg hunt and good food. The eggs are loaded with cash, candy, and slips of paper letting you draw for gift cards and prizes. Even the old guys get to revive their childhood and run over those who get in their way.

Later some chocolate bunnies will meet their doom, big ears first.

I saw a picture of people's homes in Syria recently. They were mostly concrete shells hollowed out. In Lebanon I visited refugee camps full of misery and felt the tense atmosphere in Israel and heard the mournful cry to prayers in the dark alleys of Cairo. Something made me want to go home.

Sometimes you need to go somewhere where you can look back on our planet and reflect on Good Friday and Easter and the chocolate bunnies. We take almost every good thing for granted here. I don't think a lot of the people trashing our country would be so flippant about our freedom if they had spent some time somewhere where it wasn't quite as free. You think what we've gotten at the expense of some brave human beings. You get a bit angry at people who have no grasp or care to know what the price of peace has cost others.

In Germany they once put me on a 2-year waiting list for a phone. GTE looked like all-world to me after that. We've gotten so spoiled taking blessings for routine. We assume the police will protect us, and there will be milk on the shelf or gas at the pumps down at the convenience store. I came home from overseas in the early 70's to gas lines and rationing. Welcome home. I thought I left that behind me overseas.

We get aggravated at our leaders and the increasing demands placed on us at work and at home. The pressures are greater than ever. At least here in this country we can still celebrate Easter and Christmas and the other holidays that make up the fabric of our society.

Having visited the empty churches and faded hope of the European villages, I fear we too could go the same way if we do not guard our freedom, protect our guns, and refuse to let the government take care of us until we have to. I'm fond of saying, "Ain't no free money." I also frequently repeat, "Freedom isn't free." I only hope our children and grandchildren are still willing to pay the price. To whom much is given, much is required. We have been given much.

How Do They Know

One day it was dreary gray. The next day the tulip tree said, "Time to wake up. Spring is here." How does it know when? Close on its tail are Bradford pears. It's almost like somebody went down the road touching each one almost at the same time.

The yellow and white bulbs all popped up at the same time in the beds. The wild onions and dandelions have no fear. The St. Augustine is a little more hesitant. I say grass is smarter than we are as it seems leery of that last freeze that may yet be coming.

Critters also amaze me. They honk as they head north telling us to put on the bright colors and whites. Speed up to September and you'll find a mess of doves sitting on my highline in the pasture. They show up the night before dove season opens. Now how do they know? I dipped smelt from rivers on the Canadian border as they raced each year to the ocean. How do they know?

A couple of weeks back you couldn't go down the highway without running over a dead skunk. I don't care if he is dead he still stinks up your car. It was almost as if every boy skunk in the county was in a mad dash to find a girlfriend.

Unfortunately, several were blinded by love or headlights and paid the price. It's amazing that they all knew to move almost at once. Who told them to go? A lot of deer seem to suffer similar fates crossing highways as something urges them to pursue love at all costs.

I describe a lot of these seasonal changes to ask if all this can be pure accident. It would seem that we would have to suspend our common sense that something is behind it all. Jesus once said, "I tell you that, if these should hold their peace, the stones would immediately cry out." It is a stretch to not believe that some mighty orchestrated hand is conducting a living symphony, each element coming into play at just the right moment. How can all this be random?

The popular belief about the Big Bang Theory wants us to believe in some sort of cosmic event that just happened. I'd like to believe in my universe that such an event couldn't just happen. It is a lot more comforting to think that some force or power is in control and managing it all. We're told that even the hairs on our head are numbered.

Maybe by just believing it is all random, it lets people not have to consider that someone is in control with a master plan. If there is a master plan then we have a responsibility to find out our role in the whole thing.

The challenge then becomes, "What am I here for?" It's a lot easier to just say it's all coincidental and accidental. However, if we take that route of disbelief, we could be totally missing a special plan designed for us. After all, I want to believe we rate a little higher than Bradford pears and love-struck skunks.

Sick 'Em

Most of us do pretty much what we want. We might not feel quite good enough to go to church Sunday morning, but we make a miraculous recovery and have dinner with family and friends Sunday night.

I've had people describe their struggle with life as having an angel on one shoulder and a devil on the other. Others tell me about two dogs fighting inside us – one good and one bad. When asked who wins, the person says, "Whoever I say sick 'em to."

We make a lot of stupid excuses for selfish actions. Down deep, we know it's wrong but we generally do what we want. We may feel that we've worked hard and deserve a day off even though we have no days left to use. One store clerk recently justified taking money from the store. The clerk felt a raise was due but her boss didn't agree. Cassius said to Brutus, "The fault, dear Brutus, is not in our stars, but in ourselves." We do what we want.

I think we would all be happier if we simply cut out the middleman and just said, "I did it because I wanted to." Life would be a lot less confusing if people operated like Jim Carrey's character in his movie where he could not tell a lie. I knew a strong personality once. The person lost a lot of weight and looked very nice.

A friend in a meeting sitting by both of us commented how nice the person looked. The response back was, "Yeah, but I am still a witch." I won't tell you what they said, but the other person beside me voiced agreement. It was a sad commentary on a life, but at least it was honest.

We don't like bad guys, but at least we understand where they are coming from. So-called good friends and "good" people drive us crazy when we realize they are hypocrites and have stomped on our hearts. Putin of Russia and Kim Jong-un of North Korea don't pretend to be nice. They do what they want and ask what you're going to do about it.

I wonder if bad guys who are thoroughly evil suffer any of the issues that people do who are conflicted and try to walk that thin line between good and evil. Choosing between doing good and evil is hard sometimes.

Apostle Paul said, "For that which I do I allow not; for what I would, that do I not; but what I hate, that do I." Internal conflict can be hard on the body. Timothy was Paul's protégé and a young pastor feeling the pressure. Paul told him, "Use a little wine for thy stomach's sake and thine often infirmities." For me growing up it was Pepto, Alka Seltzer, and Milk of Magnesia.

Because the pressures are only increasing, whether you're a teacher or President, people need to realize they are in a battle for control of their hearts. Jesus said, "For out of the abundance of the heart the mouth speaks." We must deny power to the things that will hurt us and pursue the things that will help us. Hopefully, less conflict, better health. Tell the good dog to sick 'em.

Lukewarm

Jesus said, "So then because thou art lukewarm, and neither cold nor hot, I will spew thee out of my mouth." I can't think of anything good to say about lukewarm. I hate warm milk, coffee, coke, Chinese food, and just about anything else to eat or drink that is lukewarm. Does anyone ever say, "I think I'll take a lukewarm bath?"

Think about people you know. Do you really look forward to conversation with a lukewarm personality? Another term for that person is "bump on a log." We like people who engage us and inspire us, who challenge us and encourage us. We like passionate people who live life with zest.

Lukewarm people come in all shapes and sizes. Some are 60 and some are 6. They may do just enough to keep their job but not enough to run the whole place. They probably won't offend any person, then again no one will probably remember them soon after they're gone.

We are not talking about bad people. We're saying we only have one life to live. We're not all gifted speakers or firebrands, but a lukewarm person is lacking that spark needed to have a life of zest and vigor. The Beetles song about Eleanor Rigby who lived an ignominious life gives a picture of a person living life in half-measures.

Marriages can be lukewarm. They become routine. Passion is replaced with ordinary. We can live in the middle of it and not recognize it or be unsure about what to do to breathe life into it.

Friendships can be lukewarm. They tend to just exist.

You want that feeling of warmth or a giggle or just a good smile down deep when you think of friends. You love the fun and the feeling of emotions or quiet pleasure you get from a friend who brings out the best in you. Because they know you so well and know the secret touchy spots, they can bring out the worst, too. A true friend knows enough to destroy you but won't. A lukewarm friend hardly seems worth the trouble at times.

Organizations can also be lukewarm. Herb Kelleher of Southwest Airlines once said in looking for a job, if you enter a place of prospective employment and do not hear laughter, turn around and look elsewhere.

Organizations have personalities like people do. You spend more time at work than at home. Don't spend your life in a place you can barely tolerate. As Herb noted, go where there is life and laughter—not lukewarm. Work where you find creative people with passion who don't just endure life, but they love life. The friendships you find there will be more than just lukewarm. They will help you develop into the person you can be.

Crossing the Line

Col. Travis drew a line with his sword at the Alamo. Those who crossed it were saying they were ready to give all for Texas. When I lived in West Germany in the early 70's brave souls in East Berlin would try to sneak across to West Berlin, usually with the same fatal results of those before them.

These lines were clearly marked. Many are not so obvious. I raised my boys to understand that we have to have an internal line that cannot be crossed. Many politicians go to Washington to do good, but along the way they become rich and jaded. The line became blurred. The bright lights of Hollywood have blinded many a young person who was willing to do what it took to be a star. Glen Campbell's song "Rhinestone Cowboy" says "There's been a load of compromising on the road to my horizon."

Crossing that line is usually a gradual thing; most girls are familiar with the hand on the knee. Most evil, most corruption, starts out slowly. Ever heard the story of the monkey in the pot of water? As the temperature was slowly increased, the monkey didn't realize his goose was cooked until it was too late.

Most of us have worked in organizations where all felt pressure to fit in; some of it was blatant and some was more subtle. It gets scary out on that limb by yourself. Most of us want to feel that we belong. We want to be liked and valued, but at what price?

Sometimes acceptance into the group can be very costly. We literally can lose ourselves.

We've all heard someone say, "I don't even recognize the person you've become." In some cases our literal appearance has changed. Ever been to a class reunion where someone got the award for "Person who has changed the most?" More often we're talking about a person's outlook or value system.

The problem with crossing that line of who we are is that it can cost us our literal soul and identity. Like a boat torn loose from its mooring, once we've been pulled out into that ocean of chaos, we're not likely to ever reach shore again. You must keep a clear picture of who you are, and pull yourself back on course when you feel like you're drifting off course.

My mother used to say to me, "Shake yourself, just shake yourself." Above all things we must strive to make sure people can see who we really are. Be like a diamond clear and brilliant. Let people always see who you are. People are uneasy with people they are not sure of.

We must be so consistent in our behavior that people can tell when we are acting out of character. We can't afford to cross that identity line that forever leads into a world where even we no longer recognize who we are.

The Smarter Sex

Since the age of 10 I've had the privilege of working with elderly widows, both in our lawn business and more recently as Visitation Pastor to our shut-ins. We had mostly widows with an occasional widower as customers. What struck me was the way in which older ladies adjusted to widowhood compared to the men.

First of all, there weren't many men to be included in my study. The same held true both in our lawn business and in observing the widows and shut-ins in our church. The women did a much better job socially than the guys. If they were a little younger and still driving cars, they often bonded together, frequently 5 or 6 in a car going to their favorite eating places.

One of my favorite ladies has survived the loss of 2 husbands and yet retained the positive, feisty position of ringleader. Her zest for life demonstrates that you can hang in there and thrive in the face of tough odds. Her group has great communication with each other and that makes it easier to help support each other. They truly understand the knowledge that there is strength in numbers. Ecclesiastes says, "A cord of 3 strands is not quickly broken."

The widowers did not seem to make the same effort to socialize; they were not willing to invest the same amount of time and activities that helped the women support each other. Again, there weren't that many elderly men to observe, which helped explain why the guys might not have the same opportunities to get together with other men.

It might also partly be explained by the fact that so much of a man's identity often revolved around his work. Women worked also, but relationships and social interaction at work and outside work took a higher priority than it did for us guys. My wife has probably a half dozen good to best friends.

She rarely lacks for someone to talk with on the phone, go eat with, or catch a movie. I don't want to take the time she does to keep up her friendships. When I get a chance to rest, I'm likely to read, watch Fox News, or take an accidental nap in the recliner.

I'm glad my wife has her network of support. A lot of older widowers I've known also have had good family support. Since I was an old soldier returning from the wars at 30 and she an 18 year old, most likely I will go first. It gives me great comfort that she has a small army of supporters who will help and encourage her during her bereavement.

Unlike her, I haven't taken the time to build up relationships with other guys which might help me get through similar times. Maybe what I'm observing is more proof that women are actually smarter than the guys.

Naw, I just think they tend to have more fun! I just wish I didn't wonder if some of those giggles may be directed at us guys!

Letting Go

After observing family life there seems to be one fight we could do without. It's common for adult kids to go home and have a feeling like being a little kid in your parents' presence. I think that's normal and helps remind us of the love and respect we've had for good parents. It's also kind of comforting to have the feeling of being home again and reviving old memories of family life.

A darker, more unnatural byproduct of growing up can be a dysfunctional relationship with one or more parents. It often falls on the parent side of the relationship. It is also the cause of the loss of a strong relationship between them and most likely the issue is rooted in an insecurity on the parent's part.

Have you experienced or observed a parent continuing to sound and act toward an adult child like he did when the now adult was under their care? The parent most likely doesn't realize what they are doing or not doing. It comes natural after 18 years and constant direction and guidance.

You were doing your best to get that kid raised and ready for the world. How do you turn it off after so many years of guidance? Power is a hard thing to give up.

We parents often say how happy we'll be when the kids are grown and on their own. The kid agrees with you. The problem now is for us parents to take on a new role. The relationship has always been adult-to-child. Now it must become adult-to-adult. As parents we have absolute control. We now have to replace that with mutual respect, no longer a one-way street. If we can't make this transition as a parent then we are going to miss some of the greatest blessings ever.

If we become less of a parent and more of a mentor, friend, and equal, we may be amazed what a good job we've done and what a good person, in spite of the times we messed up, that we've helped develop.

There are many young people who are slow to develop into adulthood. Don't give up. Like the admonition in Proverbs says, "Train up a child in the way he should go and when he is old, he will not depart from it."

Backing off and treating your adult child the way they deserve to be treated is one of the hardest things some of us will have to do. Some wise parents have been able to get a head start on developing these relationships when kids were young. It can be hard and scary to find yourself trying to give up control and trust the young adult.

It can also be a reward to see that the acorn has become a strong tree. The child carries on your legacy and trains up the next generation to come. Your guidance helped make it happen. Good job Mom and Dad!

Pat on the Back

In a recent successful political campaign my son wrote in an article that there is a special sleep that comes from earned rest compared to that of unearned rest. Along with saluting the flag and standing for the national anthem, respect for hard work and those who do it seems to have deteriorated. I'm not sure who's at fault here.

Our government has made it easier for people to reject minimum wage jobs in favor of government support. It's hard to go into a lot of the businesses in our small town without seeing a "Help Wanted" sign on the front door. There are people who have disabilities or fallen on hard times and temporarily need some help. Our community is famous for stepping up and helping people in need.

Having a job and taking pride in it helps a person feel good about themselves and their contribution to the family.

The local trash collector walked halfway down my drive to give me my trash can. He didn't have to do that. Sometimes I take him and his buddies a coke and some cookies in the hot Texas summer.

If I have several bundles of small limbs or a lot of Christmas trash, I may tape a couple of dollars onto the container. The guys help me out all the time around town as we have landscaping leftovers. They don't have to do it.

I told my boys growing up to be respectful and grateful to our waitress and lawn mower repair guy. They are the ones standing between us and hot food and equipment to do our work. I love country cafes and convenience stores that feel like home and go the extra mile to serve you.

People deserve dignity and respect, whatever their occupation. I love workers who love their work and it shows. Businesses, like people, have personalities. That atmosphere of service and pride in work has to start at the top and filter down. I will pay extra any day to go to a Mom and Pop place where they go out of their way to be hospitable.

Big box stores have their place, but it's hard for them to match the genuine appreciation a lot of smaller businesses have for their customers. Local stores continue to fall by the wayside, swept aside by the big boys. Give the local guys a pat on the back while you can.

Here's hoping that more people in businesses, big and small, can find jobs that you enjoy and take pride in. We need more businesses where employees meet you at the front door or greet you in the aisle to help you.

Loving to work and getting that earned rest at the end of your shift can add a lot to a person's satisfaction with life. You may get the same pay for doing a good job or bad one, but only you know inside how good it feels to know you've put in a good day's work for a day's pay.

Picking Up the Pieces

Ozzie and Harriet, Jim and Margaret, Ward and June—icons of simpler days—solved life's problems in thirty minutes. Today they and their trouble-free lives are hard to find, even on TV Land. I thought about those TV days where our heroes didn't ever consider or mention the big D.

My wife and I haven't either, but she said murder had crossed her mind a few times after I smarted off and acted a jerk once too often. Probably most of you guys haven't had that disease that I can't seem to get rid of—foot in the mouth.

The subject of divorce of young couples came up recently when word came of another young couple possibly throwing in the towel. The wrestling match was over. It felt like a piece of me just got removed. I'm feeling hurt for the parents and grandparents. John Donne said, "Any man's death diminishes me." Divorce is like a living death. When my high school dates' fathers in the early 60's asked what my father did for a living, I said he was dead. Divorce was uncommon back then. I often meet adults who still bear the scars divorce inflicted when they were young.

When the young couples break up you wonder what made them give up. Was it too much debt, unrealized dreams, too high expectations, or goals not reached quickly enough? Did we older guys make it look too easy? Didn't they see the long work hours and the sacrifices we made? Is sacrifice the key? Around Mother's Day Jimmy Dean does this recitation on the radio about thanking his mom for her sacrifices including giving up the last piece of pie because she said she wasn't hungry any more.

Parents have repeatedly done things like that for the kids in the past when a parent's secretly harbored desire had to wait a while – maybe a newer truck or remodeling the kitchen, or a trip to somewhere. America has been blessed as individuals and as a country way beyond what we deserve. Like Ozzie and Harriet did, parents have made sure the kids got the clothes they needed or that bike they just had to have.

A friend of mine in Germany had a house full of kids. Even his officer's pay was stretched thin. One day the teen daughter threw a fit about having to ride to school in an older car. She was so embarrassed and asked her mom why they couldn't have a new car like her friends. Her mother pointed at the braces on her teeth and said, "There's your new car." Parents love their kids and would do whatever it takes because they want to feel like the Cleavers, Nelsons, and Andersons who seemed to have it all, even though Ward, Jim, and Ozzie didn't have to pull an extra shift, overtime, or second job to do it.

I want all of us parents to think about the sacrifices you made as you loved your kids and did everything you could to show them how much you cared for them. We did all we could to show them what love in action looks like. 1st Timothy 5:8 said, "If any provide not for his own he has denied the faith, and is worse than an infidel."

With my dad leaving us as kids, I think I vowed to be twice as good a dad to help make up for my father's absence in our lives. Parents don't need to feel guilty when their children divorce. Our generation did everything we could to help prepare them for a successful life. Divorce was not in the plan. Now, many parents and grandparents have to take on an extra role of providing extra support for the family broken by divorce.

Parents and grandparents do what they do best. They help pick up the pieces, give aid to the wounded, and help the kids and grandkids start over again. Optimists know the sun will shine again. There's no place for guilt in this scenario. Everyone is too busy helping pull things together, one school pickup and one more soccer practice at a time. All hands on deck!

House or Home

If "clothes make the man," then does the house make the home? If we "dress for success," does our house help ensure happiness. These old phrases probably haven't had much effect on my career over the years. In a small town people pretty much accept you as you are.

A wealthy friend of mine whose family has worldwide holdings told me she was asked by an affluent friend why they still made their headquarters here. She said, "I like a small town. The good thing about it is that you know everyone. The bad thing is everybody knows you." So you become a big duck in a little pond much like Cheers where everyone knows your name, but they still treat you like one of the guys.

Recently as I crisscrossed the county putting up campaign signs for my son I got a good look at each nook and cranny. I could not believe how many people lived on the county roads. I also couldn't believe the sheer number of beautiful country homes, many of them newly constructed.

I visited with Californians relocating here fleeing the high cost of taxes and real estate. I can estimate house prices; somebody has hit it big, or someone has a big house payment. Even at 4% or less it's still a challenge. Throw in a nice pickup and SUV in the driveway, and you can imagine the monthly income needed to keep the wolf away from the door.

You have to believe there are some fearless people out there living the American dream. Waylon Jennings used to sing about "four-car garage and we're still building on." There are some advantages to being younger and full of optimism. They believe they will have the income to get 'er done. They are willing to back their ears and jump in head first. Our economy is driven by home-building; when it slows down, so does the stock market and the job market.

I think I'm glad no one told me I couldn't do it. It's nice to be ignorant and not know any better. What I saw in the country mirrored the general optimism of much of our country. I saw really nice places with stables of horses and corrals for roping. I saw dreams coming alive. Four wheelers dotted the landscape. People weren't just getting by. They looked prosperous. The new homes in town and on the outskirts mirrored the country.

We old timers know life ebbs and flows. Sometimes for sale signs have covered the countryside. Lately it's a tight market with low inventory. A lot of us have learned that neither new clothes nor big new houses can ensure happiness. A house is merely a house.

The challenge is to take the empty building and make it a living, breathing place where your kids' friends and even strangers can feel that it is not just a pretty place but a haven from all the hubbub and noise around us.

Living and Dying

Somebody once told me that old age is not for sissies. It often feels like we're in a war with our bodies. My newest VA doctor recently asked if I had ever had skin cancer, and I said no. His response was, "You will." I know we're not going to get out of this world alive, short of the Rapture. It gets a little frustrating waiting to see what the next ailment will be coming along.

In Sunday school I go around the room getting updates and new diagnoses before I start the lesson. We get prayer and praise reports for our class and learn about others who have been blessed or are facing new challenges. It seems that the sharing helps ease our burdens as others lift us up.

Recently we sang Happy Birthday to a member who wasn't there as he fought to stay positive and not give up. His wife loved it and passed it along. Our heart is often stronger than the rest of the body. It fights to hang in there but you get so tired.

Have you ever felt a prisoner in your own body? The bladder can constantly interrupt your sleep and make an out-of-town trip risky. Then ye olde colon has to have its say about who runs the show. I keep reminding my class that a new body comes with the next phase of our life. Some days that's about all you have to hang onto in the middle of this aging warfare.

This can be depressing if we let it. On the other hand it's kind of fun to look at old age and say, "Is that all you got? Give me your best shot!" The recliner, couch, and bed are our enemies. They want to slowly, sneakily draw us in to giving up to the pain.

The pain, coward of cowards, wants to stop us. Instead, you and I have to do what we can and accept what we can't. We don't have to stop everything we enjoy. Some things can still happen but just take longer or require a slower pace.

You have to watch yourself and your friends as they start going to bed earlier or sleeping later than usual. In Christian terms we say the Devil can't steal our salvation, but he can take our joy and leave us just struggling to hang in there.

Old Mr. Depression wants to do something similar. He wants to take the joy out of the time we have left. Ephesians tells us, "Therefore be careful how you walk, not as unwise men but as wise, making the most of your time, because the days are evil."

When we are young we see life as an artesian well that will never run dry. In time we learn the truth. As early as the year 1225 AD there was a phrase that said, "Time and the tide wait for no man." We can accept our fate and fight on or give up. We can choose how we want to use our time remaining. Red, in the movie <u>Shawshank Redemption</u> said it best – "Get busy living or get busy dying." I think I choose living.

Work and Friends

Even now as I write this post old friends chime in with thoughts. Each one brings a whole new set of memories that oddly enough go back to work situations. When you think how much more time we spend at work verses being with family at home, it's no wonder that so many of our adult friendships began in the workplace.

One old friend reminded me recently on Facebook of our summer spent building the Civic Center and then building his house after work. Another couple of guys mentioned about the coal mine days we worked out at Thermo. Another friend who just retired as President of Eastern New Mexico University, recently sparked memories of minimum wage at Texas Tech Student Union.

At least wearing the bow tie, cummerbund, and little red jacket while serving the Governor or other dignitaries did enable us to pig out later on leftover steak and strawberry shortcake. I felt badly about missing the cauliflower and mystery meat back in the dorm cafeteria.

Riding in a Cajun pirogue in the Atchaflaya Swamp with those wild Louisiana boys grabbing water moccasins by the tail and snapping off their heads like Lash Larue will help you make friends quickly. Planting electronic jugs among the alligators to help us locate oil has a way of getting guys to cover each other's backs.

A lot of us found lifelong friendships in the military. My best man was a wild child who under the influence of something in Germany leapt off a second story balcony. He said his parachute didn't open. Looking back maybe his elevator didn't go all the way to the top either. He recovered, helped me get married, and went on to get his doctorate as a Presbyterian minister.

My ninth grade General Science teacher couldn't say "Juan;" there were no Hispanics in Sulphur Springs then. My friend Oscar Aguilar's family came later. Oh could Mrs. Aguilar cook that Mexican sweet treat bunuelos. It was not on the menu—looked like a sopapilla on steroids. Anyway, Mr. Rawson called me "Guam" for a year. I didn't have the heart or bravado to correct him.

Joe Bob Burgin and I spent some good times working in the snack bar of the Hi-Vue drive-in theater, best food in the world. Charles and Lewis Helm, following in Punk's shoes, were young business boys bringing cotton candy out there for us to sell.

Farmers Co-op was the training ground for a lot of us young guys. Aaron McKenzie, Doyle's dad, would let me work into the night unloading boxcars. That overtime helped me through college in Lubbock.

Audley, Sonny, and Joe Moore's construction company also helped this poor boy through school. They took me into the office in the almost completed Ocean Spray in cold December on a school break. They promised me work anytime I needed it. True to their word, on rainy days I cleaned concrete forms or other less glamorous jobs. I was proud to have friends who cared about me as an employee and a person.

The world of work has probably provided a lot of you with some great friends. It might be that misery loves company, but more than likely friendships at work was one of the things that helped make the time more bearable, and don't tell our bosses, but at times almost enjoyable.

Perfection

Ever thought how a grandbaby changes everything. Most Friday nights we call out to the country and offer a bribe of a free dinner somewhere if they will let us come babysit. I can't use that term "bribe" after January when he is Judge. There's no need for subtlety here; we want to come play with the critter that didn't exist a year ago outside her mommy's tummy. We watch her do sign language and listen to her new words. She has to be one of the smartest kids ever. Then I am humbled after learning that Clay's friend has a daughter who already knows some Spanish at 15 months. Clay, we've got work to do.

I love the way Gus the guard dog and all around farm protector steps between the grandbaby and us if he thinks she's threatened. She's got her own Secret Service. The cat mouse catcher and snake scarer offer defers to the child by ignoring an occasional grab from the little hand. I think I heard the mama cat say, "My bad." Hate to tell her but the kid thing only gets worse, especially if Emmie becomes big sister. Better run for your life while you can.

I try to compete for her attention, but Mamaw is winning hands down. Maybe I will have a shot later when I can take her to the Mcdonalds playground and Kid Kingdom and fishing at the pond with her Barbie fishing pole. The grandbaby holds out her arms to Mamaw. I pretend not to be jealous; I know she's invested time in building up a relationship with her since birth.

Today we're in Oklahoma at a really neat petting zoo with tons of birds, snakes, goats, sheep, llamas, donkeys, fawns, grown deer, and a myriad of other creatures. An employee says the menagerie changes daily as people drop off orphans and

81

unwanted pets. Emmie took up with the goats and a pony. The little cow from India kept insisting that she feed her.

A doe that had been raised there and released came back last night, jumped the fence, and delivered twins. Mama and twins are fine. Thank goodness she had been attending a deer yoga class to maintain flexibility.

This afternoon Emmie is sitting in the cold, clear brook full of small fish and crawdads. She keeps making sounds of delight serving as words as the fish nibble at her and run for their lives. Her cries of protest after being pulled from the stream are quickly quelled by some kind of cheese puffs or snow pea. I knew she took after me.

Back in the cabin we're getting sleepy as she focuses on Peppa Pig, the English cartoon. I had no clue, but she loves her and has since birth. Mickey's Playhouse is a close second. What a great excuse to just sit with baby in lap and exercise no brain cells. At 18 months grandson Shiloh sat behind us and spent most of his flight time to Hawaii watching a video game narrated by two silly English guys who are making a fortune.

This all reminds me now how much we came to learn on Sesame Street all those years on PBS. Bert and Ernie almost became members of the family.

She's asleep now. Mama and Daddy are out running around the Oklahoma hills doing what young ones do on vacation while the grandfolks stand watch, baby monitor and all. It's a tough job , but somebody's got to do it. The kids get a chance for some great alone time, and we get to practice spoiling the baby.

After all, practice makes perfect. We all know Emmie doesn't have far to go to reach perfection, all prejudice aside.

Old Yellow and the Boys

My El Camino and I have celebrated 35 years together. Old Yellow has been a faithful friend and has achieved minor celebrity status , being featured in political commercials for my son's successful pursuit of the judge position. Earlier it was featured in the state championship football program since head coach Greg's nickname is El Camino. The last I heard, my wife plans to bury me in it. I've told several people inquiring about buying it to watch the obituaries; she may change her mind if they make her a good enough offer.

Sadly some of us may have spent more time with our mechanical buddies than with our wives. We pat em and talk to em. We're amazed at their dependability. We're recognized when we drive em. They become a part of our persona. On different occasions both sons have made references in speeches, social media, and books they've written mentioning the man in the yellow El Camino. When they were in high school, I had different levels of punishment, all involving Old Yellow, if they got into trouble.

Level 1 was them driving the empty truck to school; Level 2 was me driving them to school in it; Level 3 was me driving them there with it loaded with our lawn equipment. My wife had a similar experience in high school as her banker and good deal finder dad came to pick her up in an old fashioned Cadillac he had bought while her secret crush and high school hunk standing nearby yelled, "Check it out. It's the Munsters." I think the reference to our ride had something to do with Sanford and Son.

In time it all turned around.

In law school Clay would come home on break and take local girls out in it, running up and down Gilmer and Broadway like I did years ago in the 57 Chevy. I started to name names of you guys I used to see out there, but my list got too long. You know who you are. When I asked Clay what the deal was about his dating technique, he said, "Dad, if they are too good to run around with me in the El Camino, then they're too good for me." What a test. To my knowledge , no girls turned him down. That is a grounded guy. Can't you hear the music as Fred drives up.

Have you ever noticed how us guys like to fix up our trucks and modify them to make them personalized. We stick on decals and other stickers. I put a Texas Tech license plate holder and double T on the back of Old Yellow. That could go along with the tee shirt my staff gave me years ago which read, "Education pays if you have a lawn mower." Earlier they gave me a shirt that said, "I fought the lawn and the lawn won." I always tell people when it comes to what matters, "Your friends care about you in spite of you.

The others won't be there when the going gets tough." Lawn mowing let me stay in one town and not have to get caught up in the superintendent merry-go-round. When a nearby town of moderate size asked me to be their superintendent, my oldest son had left Texas to play college baseball in Virginia, but my youngest still had 3 years in high school. I told him we would have to move to take the job.

He said, "Dad, I'd like to graduate here." I said, OK, we'll just keep on mowing." I never regretted that decision. The opportunity to spend time working with both sons as they were growing up was like a dream come true.

Maybe because my dad wasn't around after we left the farm was the reason that I doubly valued time with my sons. It will always be one of the greatest blessings to get to teach them how to work and the importance of visiting with our little widow lady customers after mowing while I finished trimming. The El Camino was the constant presence in this stage of their lives.

I feel like Old Yellow was like a fourth member of our team as they worked to help me be able to support my family in a small town. I had seen the world and chose to come home. Mowing also helped me pursue my love for teaching and yet give us a good life with the extras to help them have all the opportunities to pursue whatever dream they chose to follow. Each boy at different times used their landscaping skills to help support themselves.

The Bible says, "Raise up a child in the way he should go and when he is old he will not depart." I believe Old Yellow deserves part of the credit for being a faithful enabler in helping each boy find his way into manhood and independence.

Magnet and Steel

On Father's Day the boys sent me best wishes and I sent similar ones to them. It's just another reminder how blessed I've been. I try to be grateful and frequently say thank you for my blessings, but I get complacent and take things and people for granted like we all do sometimes.

Do you ever consider how we are constantly bombarded with blessings we never think about. We have unlimited clean drinking water while religious organizations raise funds to drill water wells for parched people overseas. People line up in foreign countries for food donated by other countries while Americans battle increasing obesity. Light switches give us light; air conditioners in our cars and homes make Texas heat bearable. We choose from a myriad of television and internet providers. Many times our biggest fights are over where to go eat.

Sunday mornings we head to church. We're free to assemble and encourage one another and receive a blessing that will help strengthen us until we meet again. There is a reason why Paul tells us, "Not forsaking the assembling of ourselves together, as is the manner of some, but exhorting one another, and so much the more, as ye see the day approaching." I know I am weak and need all the help I can get. I try to visit our shut-ins monthly so that they don't feel abandoned. It's easy for us to do as we often find ourselves in a whirlwind of activity and forgetting those old saints who served as role models for us for so long.

Every Sunday you could count on them being in their place and all was right with the world. Today we are becoming them; soon we will become the ones at home watching services on tv. We have to remember that what goes around comes around. Maybe the better words are, "Do unto others what you would have them do unto you."

Those are tough words and hard to live by.

What has made and continues to make America the apple of the world's eye is not only its material riches with which it has been blessed but the freedom we offer everyone to succeed or fail. We've opened our arms to people willing to work hard and help make America a great country over the years.

The challenge for us as with Europe is to balance our needs as a country with the desires of millions to be a part of our blessed life. The population of here and Europe is getting older with a need to find younger workers as our economy is booming. It's hard to blame people living in poverty and unsafe conditions for wanting to find a better place. The challenge for us as a country will be to balance our needs and still have control of our borders and our nation's security.

Everywhere you look we see help wanted signs. We need people to pour concrete and roof buildings. There are crops of fruit in valleys that need harvesting. What we need is an efficient system to match our needs with the supply of labor. We have made mistakes in the past, but we are a great country that can figure out a solution to our current problems.

Without borders we are no longer a country. Without workers our economy stops. We can get it done. Our prosperity is the magnet that draws the steel of millions seeking the blessings we often take for granted. I'll take our problems over theirs.

A Lasting Legacy

Sometimes at funerals or listening to obituaries on the radio or seeing them in the paper, I try to figure out what this person will be remembered for. What will be their legacy? Most of the time we think of this as something materially left behind.

Lasting legacies tend to be memories of a life well lived. We name buildings, parks, and streets after people. Sooner or later people will not remember or know where the building or road got its name unless the person was nationally known.

One of the best known locations for recognition in television, movies, theater, music, and radio is located in Hollywood, California. Some honored have even included Mickey Mouse and Lassie. Some get to see their star on the Walk of Fame before they die. For others it is a posthumous honor. The world of entertainment sees the honor of a star as part of their legacy to the world. Fame is fleeting. In time the mention of their name will evoke the question, "Who?

Most colleges, professional teams, and many high schools have plaques, jerseys, statues, and other forms of recognition of star athletes of the past. They may be recognized by a local or national hall of fame. Some honored athletes go on to own local or national businesses partly built on their fame.

The legacies that most of us encounter are in our families, friends, and ourselves. The legacies that matter the most are the ones you and I leave behind for them. Having money, stock, land, and other things left to us is nice. A legacy full of great memories, loving actions, and a name based on quality living often outlives any materials bequeathed us or our families.

Some people believe in waiting until their death to materially benefit or bless beneficiaries when such help might have had greater benefit when beneficiaries were younger and needier.

A nonmaterial legacy is something a person can share throughout a lifetime of positive examples and loving actions. It can't be given over to another person in a letter from a lawyer or a reading of the will. The legacy left behind that matters is one witnessed from childhood. It's the one we acquired by observation and interaction with our benefactor. It was the legacy of love shown in action, kindness demonstrated, and forgiveness given.

As He prepared to die, Jesus described the legacy of the Holy Spirit He was leaving, "Nevertheless I tell you the truth; it is expedient for you that I go away: for if I go not away, the Comforter will not come unto you; but if I depart, I will send Him unto you."

The legacy of the Holy Spirit left behind for Christians is far more valuable than any material things. It is a spiritual GPS to help us find and maintain the right path in life. As in all things in life, the gift is only as valuable as we integrate it into our lives. May we value the price of the legacy that was given to us when Christ made the ultimate sacrifice.

Hope Springs Eternal

At this writing in Thailand countries have sent help to try and rescue a group of boys trapped in a cave. In 2010 the world responded to rescue 33 miners from a mine in Chile. Whether it is a tsunami or earthquake, we see barriers dropped as the best in mankind demonstrates what can be accomplished when we work together.

There is no secret that a climate of conflict exists throughout the world. Countries struggle to control borders as refugees flee famine, danger, have a desire for increased opportunity. Have-nots seek to become haves. Aging countries and states struggle to find laborers to pick fruit, milk cows, drive trucks, provide healthcare, and teach our children. Our prosperity has created its own unique set of needs and concerns. We need roofers and construction workers and landscapers, but we struggle to meet the demand. Several friends of mine own trucking companies and can't find drivers as many of their trucks sit idle. Some have tried to train untrained drivers. They say they can't compete with wages in the oil patches paid to drivers.

We're talking about a good problem of prosperity in our country. When a country becomes prosperous people are able to focus on things other than just meeting basic needs. Maslow's hierarchy of needs goes from basic needs to self-actualization. As more people climb the ladder to success, people focus on quality of life, equality of opportunity for all, and finding personal satisfaction in our lives.

Past research has found that satisfaction rises until salaries reach a certain level. At the time the magic amount in America was about $70,000. After that, job and life satisfaction did not grow proportionally to further increases in incomes.

What we know is that serving others makes you happier. I gave a number of examples of this in my 2014 book <u>Serving Happiness</u>. The more we serve ourselves the emptier and more frustrated we become as material gains don't make us happy. Follow the lives of John Bulushi, Michael Jackson, Prince, Kurt Cobain, Marilyn Monroe, and the list goes on.

If people will look around for opportunities to make life better for others, our country and our world would become better places to live as people work together to address famine, poverty, and peace in warring countries. Hope springs eternal in the human breast.

Little Things

Trace Adkins had a country song " She Thinks We're Just Fishing." He talks about the special times they shared doing something they enjoyed. Parenting is like panning for gold. Those quality times together are like nuggets. With my eldest it was playing catch. To this day I keep two gloves and a ball in the closet. Whenever he could spare the time he'd say, "Dad, let's go play catch." We would go outside, and I would listen as we went over things on his mind.

As he got up into high school and college baseball and travelling around the world playing, I was taking my life into my hands. A ninety mile per hour fastball that moves is tough! Mostly he was kind and took it easy, but sometimes he forgot and cut loose with a doozie. Fortunately I only had an occasional bruise or red hand to show for it.

My youngest chose shooting baskets, mostly HORSE, on the driveway. It was less painful than fastballs. He is less of a talker, so I had to be especially attentive when he spoke. Neither boy was inclined to say negative things about people, better than their dad, so we talked a lot about ideas and later about cases he was trying as a prosecutor. He would try arguments out on me or ask my opinion as I acted as a member of a potential jury to see how I might see things. It was fun being a guinea pig for him to bounce ideas off of as he prepared cases.

My wife has been a different story. I don't know where the snuggling and cuddling went, but somewhere along the way she switched ends of the couch, and her feet ended up in my lap. It became foot rubs complete with baby lotion, leg massages, and occasional hand rubs. As time has gone on, these feet and back rubs have become expressions of affection.

It could be romantic but relaxation is apparently tied to the sleepy bone which leads to snoring. Like I said, priorities change as we get older. She says it's my fault that I have great hands! At least we get a little time to go over her day and hear funny things kids have said or done at school that could have been on Art Linkletter's Kids Say the Darndest Things TV show.

My little dog of 18 years died a few years back. To fill the void my neighbor's dog has a regular routine where he comes over, knocks me aside as we enter from the garage, and waits patiently for me to get him some bread. Then he heads to the front door for me to let him out and toss him the bread. He is a pig and will pull this routine as often as he can.

As I size things up I must be a soft touch, even for the neighbor's dog. Looking back on my life it's funny to see how many different ways we can find to interact with others. I think I finally came to the conclusion that you take what they give you. You meet a need of someone else, even the neighbor's dog, and along the way they help meet your need to be needed.

Singer Kitty Kallen used to sing a song called, "Little Things Mean A lot." When you get down to it, the important things in life are a series of little things that in the end mean everything.

Necessity: Mother of Invention

I was talking with my son in California the other day about how to approach a problem as a small business owner. I told him how some big hospital bills when he was a baby led me to start a side business to pay them off as his mother had to give up her job to stay home with him. The lemons became lemonade as it enabled us to do more and have more while letting my wife become a stay-at-home mom.

Second chapter happened when friends asked my wife to keep their kids during the day since she was already home. Thus began a daycare complete with house renovations to accommodate it. It grew and followed us to a larger home where we started over again with more renovation. It lasted until the boys were in school, and I had lined my wife up with a schedule and adviser in the education department over at old ETSU. No more business major, but now Early Childhood due to her successful years in her daycare. More lemons turned in to lemonade.

I reminded my son of a challenge we faced after we decided to build a larger house. Things were fine as we wrapped up construction only to have one more round of bills when we thought we were basically done. For a young couple already up to our gills in obligations it was a tough pill to swallow. And swallow we did as we scrambled to get it done. Lessons learned. We made it through the fire of inexperience and survived.

Have you ever thought about the times you grew and were able to accomplish more or deal with hardships you couldn't imagine coping with. If we had a choice most of us would skip the challenges and hardships. Fortunately or unfortunately we don't get choices sometimes. We do get a choice as to how we react to hardship. I reminded my son you grow in the valley, not on the mountaintop.

In Christian terms I've talked to people about being involuntary Bibles for the world to see. They make much better sermons. As friends have lost children and spouses they become role models for us weaker folks to see how you can make it through the valley of the shadow of death.

A dairy farmer friend who let me court three of his daughters, none of whom took, once said as he eyeballed me as a part of his future plans, "Anyone can make money in a dairy in the good times." He said the hard times are what separate the men/women from the boys.

The beauty and the cruelty of America for all of us is that we are free to tackle anything we want if we think we're big enough. Sometimes we win; sometimes we lose. Let's pray we don't ever lose the opportunity to choose in the good ole U.S. of A.

One Thing

My grandson in San Diego attends a French school all day, has piano on Wednesdays and karate three other days during the week. He did soccer for a while but it gave way to busting boards. I think a kid can get too busy and not have time to be a kid. We had to say no to year round baseball for his dad at one time. We went through karate, basketball, soccer, tennis, baseball, guitar, track, piano and I can't remember what else. I told them we didn't live for practices, so make sure you really wanted to do it. We found the money and got them there.

I've often told parents that anything is cheaper than jail when it comes to raising kids. I always told my co-workers over the years that the difference between rich kids and poor kids is opportunity. That guided much of what we did in my schools as we had jump rope team, piano classes, strings program, choir, art classes and the list goes on. We provided opportunities with the help of the community. Our scores topped out and attendance peaked. Kids had a reason to come to school. Billy Crystal asked Jack Palance in City Slickers the secret to happiness. Jack said, "One thing." Billy asked, "What?" Jack said, "That's for you to find out."

All of us parents and grandparents want our offspring to find that one thing. One of my sons followed my love of baseball that took me around the world and let me play until my legs got old. His talent took him through college and places I dreamed of. My youngest son had a million interests in the shadow of his brother's athletic accomplishments. He found his place in law and politics.

The word I'm looking for is opportunity.

We make a lot of our own opportunities, but you just can't beat good old luck and great timing. I always heard that success occurs when preparation meets opportunity. Did you ever notice how much talent is just sitting out there? I'm a testimony to a poor boy who worked hard and was blessed by a lot of people to help me along my way. Ever notice how people love to get behind a person who is trying and wants to do better than the situation they've come from. The world is a sucker for an underdog. Something in us just loves to help people out. We love how it brings the good in us out.

Anything we can do to help somebody who wants to change or do better, the key being "wants to," we need to do it. If a child shows interest—follow up on it. You'll kick yourself later if you don't. Looking back I don't regret the extra jobs and long hours it took to get it all done. On my 60th birthday my co-workers made me sit down at 8 in the morning in my office and watch a surprise birthday video.

I did fine until they got to the scene where my JAG son from some air base overseas said some nice things concluding with, "You did it right, Dad." What grace and blessings have filled my life. Snotty nose and all, that's the kind of report card we all pray for. I think he was being far too generous.

A Reason To Smile

I'm sure people get tired of my harping on the blessings in my life, but sometimes I feel like a certain famous person who tells Americans that we are going to win so much that we're going to be sick of winning. I read about some guy recently winning two different lotteries almost back to back.

I think I'd check that guy out for having an inside track or at least a four-leaf clover in his pocket. Just kidding, but can you imagine that . In me, you're looking at a guy whose biggest prize he ever won was an Evergreen feed cap at a livestock show. Don't buy me a scratch off. Now my wife's a different story. She has the touch. Maybe I actually do since I found my wife at a Ranger ballgame.

Maybe it's because I've had the opportunity to walk among the refugee camps and had hordes of begging kids surround me in places you could hardly breathe due to the stench of burning garbage. Maybe it was spending time in countries where even getting basic necessities were not a given.

Before long you almost get paranoid wondering if you'll ever get back to good old normal USA. Back then I hit the States at the end of the Vietnam era and was greeted by gas shortages and long lines. Somehow as I picked my car up from the ship in the New Jersey harbor, I didn't even mind it because I was home again. The sound of the word made me smile.

I couldn't get enough hamburgers and French fries and real Coke and milkshakes. I didn't even mind stopping here for ten gallons of gas here and five gallons there. At least I could afford to buy it. That wasn't always true in places I had been.

Now after years of being gone from home, I stopped off to see my mom on the way to a job, got a different job, got a wife and got a life I never dreamed of or planned on. I think they call it putting down roots. It's a mixture of debts and promises to pay; it's building a name and leaving a legacy; it's finding a steeple with other sinners under it who know they, too, have been blessed and forgiven; it's finding old and new friends to enrich your life and comfort you and yours in death; it's a sense of belonging, even when you get older, and you think no one remembers you. They do.

The funeral may be small, but the impact you leave is great. I always told my coworkers and students over the years to make it their goal to be irreplaceable. Call it job security. Do anything and everything to make the place a success. They will soon realize you're too valuable to let go.

An old cowboy friend once said ,"When you look back and see the trail you rode , does it make you smile to think of the stops along the way and the blessings you shared? If you can, congratulations on a life well lived. If you can't, get busy on it." I say better late than never.

Time

It was just about as good a bachelor night as you can get. The wife was out of state with a new grandson. I'm sitting in front of the TV watching <u>Gunsmoke</u>, a can of viennie sausages open, a stack of crackers, and some pork and beans in a can. I wish I could find Campbells, but I have to settle for Van Camps. No need for dishes here, just some plastic utensils from Braum's. Throw in some sweet pickles and you get a pauper's feast. Look ma, no dishes to wash.

True, I'm sleeping on the couch for two weeks because the bed is too big. I can stand it if I don't unmake her side of the bed. Then I can lean up against her pillow sham and pretend she's there. I still can't feel her foot as my right foot reaches out in vain. Nope. It's back to the couch. At least my foot won't have any room for foot reaching.

None of you have ever, but we play the snoring game. The goal is to be the first one to go to sleep. The winner can tune out the noise of the other. The loser gets to lie there awake and be jealous. It gets worse if you have to get up in the wee hours and wee wee . If you can keep your eyes closed and feel your way to the commode, you've got a good chance to get right back at it. If you are unfortunate enough to accidentally catch your little toe on the corner of a cabinet or trim, you are now awake and in pain. You're praying the toe isn't broken or missing a toenail.

Back in bed you start going over every stupid possibility of life, death, taxes, bankruptcy, and anything else to guarantee you're awake for a while. Ever notice how those dark hours just before dawn are either the deepest sleep or the darkest time of worry. Once the sun starts coming up, the cowardly fears and worries seem to recede and laugh at us for foolishly giving worry control of the night. Christians feel guilty for letting something take their joy. Others simply get aggravated and wonder if it was something they ate.

I'm glad for the moment that this short stint of bachelorhood has an end in sight. I get a little peak into the world of the widow and widower where eating and sleeping alone are obstacles to tackle daily, hopefully with an occasional reassurance that the nightmare of loneliness will give way to a light of hope. In the morning you get up and fake it until you can make it. Most people have their own trouble and don't really want an answer to, "How are you doing?"

They want you to say, "Fine." This frees them momentarily from feeling guilty about their normal life complete with spouse. Maybe a friend who is in the same boat can just smile, hug you, and let their eyes tell you that they, too, have been through the same valley of the shadow of death and survived. It ain't no fun being a member of this club. You didn't apply, and you would gladly have passed on membership.

It's not what happens to you, people say. They say it's how you react to it. You haven't read the human book of life that might have prepared you for it. Unfortunately, like being married and raising children, they haven't written one that adequately prepares you for it.

Hopefully you can reach out and touch a family member or close friend when the anesthesia of shock wears off and the raw feelings are in need of a balm. Whatever it takes, do it or use it to get through the blue days. Precious time. In time you will survive. The key is time.

No Substitute for Class

Ever had a friend that made you smile just thinking about 'em? Mine was Dan James. You can Google him and find he was a three-star general as commander of the Air National Guard of the U.S. Google his dad, Chappy James, and you'll find him as a Tuskegee Airman and highest ranking African American general in the Air Force at that time.

That's the data but not the man. He was a fighter pilot in Vietnam. He dislocated my jaw when both of us were chasing a fly ball in a game for the Air Force in windy New Mexico.. We were the odd couple; he was tall and solid like an oak tree, while I was vertically challenged, almost needing a pillow to look out the windshield of the plane. Picture Andy and Barney or Hawkeye and Radar O'Reilly.

It was 1967 in summer camp and 115 degrees on the flight line. We had made it through survival training, not sure which was worse, the fried lizard or the canned junk that could have passed for the cottonseed meal we fed to our cows. He and I became regulars on our off time in Alamogordo, Red River, and Cloudcroft. I got to watch Dan under a lot of different situations. He was always class with what they called great military bearing.

It wasn't until he asked me to be his roommate that I got to know the private Dan.

Deep into the night we talked about the pressure he experienced being the son of a famous African American general of legendary status. The stress of the Air Force Academy and his father's high expectations in the mid 60's became too much. He finished at Arizona. I lost track of him in Vietnam as he stayed busy as a fighter pilot, but one day I heard on the news that Dan had been appointed commander of the Air National Guard in Texas.

Some time later an old military veteran friend of mine told me that Dan was nominated to command the Air National Guard for the country. He thought I should holler at Dan. I did but had to leave a message. Dan was in Washington awaiting Senate confirmation and his promotion to three star general. The phone rang at work. My secretary told me a Danny James was on the line. I said I didn't know any Danny James, thinking he was a salesman. Anyway, I quickly figured it out and took the call.

We had a great visit. He asked if there was anything he could do for me. I told him about an issue regarding my son's knee from high school soccer that was holding up his Air Force scholarship to the University of Texas. He said," I don't have any kids of my own. Let me call Colorado and see what I can do. After all, what's a general for?" A week later the scholarship came through. It could have been coincidence, but I will just say, "Thanks Dan."

Dan left us recently. When I think of him I see class. In summer camp in the 60's he got the second highest award. The entire camp knew he should have gotten first. With total grace he never flinched.

In 1967 Dan demonstrated the qualities a person could use to rise above unfairness to reach the top of his profession. He taught me that the greatest revenge is success. Later in my military career I met his dad while on active duty. I could see why he held his father Chappy James in such high esteem. The apple didn't fall far from the tree. Class is class, no two ways about it.

Respite

"Shut the door. Were you born in a barn!" The truth is I purty near was. Dr. Farrington came out from Alba and delivered me on about the spot of the original AJ's Fish restaurant on 17. The minute we moved out of the two room shack with a dog run between, they started stacking hay in there. We only had a small shed for milking a few head, so it must have been cheaper than building a new barn. I remember that dog run hall because I got my head stuck in a milk can there.

My parents were actually intelligent people; not sure about the offspring. I only wanted to hear how my voice sounded inside a milk can. The smell of old milk was my punishment. That's the same head I landed on at age four when Coalie the draft horse that could sit 6 grownups on his back at one time decided to lean over and eat some grass, shooting me forward like a cleanly shelled pea.

I was reminded of these early farm days when I was out in the country at my kids. We sent them off to Commerce to eat Chinese while we watched Peppa Pig, the English cartoon phenom, with Emmie. Soon she was bundled inside her sleep sack. I joined the dogs and cats outside as dusk was turning into darkness. The quiet almost hurt my ears. I couldn't hear Matt Dillon or Vanna turning the clicking wheel.

As I walked around I was struck by the peacefulness of a working farm. Over here was the big tractor with hay fork attached; over there was the old Ford tractor backed into the shed. A cow was bawling for her calf in a nearby pen. The hay barn in the pasture was bulging with big rolls of hay that grow only more valuable as the drought drags on. The dump truck and the low boy sat ready for work, as did the work trucks.

The idle and permanently empty dairy barn was reminiscent of the 700 dairy days smaller herds and barns in our county. Now it houses exercise equipment and weights for my kids' outdoor cross fit workout area. There would be no shortage of tractor tires around here to jump off and on.

As I sat in the yard swing I caught a glimpse of new trails and fading ones in the sky made by a jet reminding me of my youth and Air Force days. The neighbor's dog kept trying to grab my crackers and cheese until I hurt his feelings. The mama cat kept harassing crickets as she occasionally pounced on them. The cars on the highway passed with a low sound, but the 4WD pickups with big rumbling tires gave off intimidating whines as if they were in pursuit of game.

Looking up I caught sight of dove lined up on nearby high line wires hoping to avoid being eaten over Labor Day. No jalapenos filled with cream cheese for their dry breasts wrapped in bacon.

For a few moments I forgot about keeping my lawn edged and trimmed because my city neighbors had already done theirs.

I was sitting on a few hundred acres of Bermuda listening to the coyotes howl and yip yip off in the pasture. For a brief respite from the sounds of traffic and sirens in the city, my body relaxed and soaked up the moment. In the morning once again the hay would fly as tractor wheels rolled. All hands on deck.

Wings and Halos

I was a bachelor until I was thirty. I had no plan. Apparently someone else did. A trip to Ranger Stadium and I met her. Forty-three years later I wish I could say it has all been smooth sailing but I'd be lying. It was probably made worse by thirty years of doing what I wanted. Bachelorhood will make you selfish.

Marriage is an almost impossible institution. Put two people together with totally different personalities and expect there to be smooth sailing---right.

Two roommates in college is bad enough. When the honey begins to dry up and the moon begins to dim, the hard work begins. God created man and then woman as a helpmate. He said it is not good for man to be alone. He has plans he wants accomplished. He gives us a set period of time to accomplish them. Job said, "A man's days are numbered.

You know the number of his months. He cannot live longer than the time you have set." We have a team and we have goals. Matthew says, "At the resurrection people will neither marry nor be given in marriage; they will be like the angels in heaven."

We work our darndest to make good marriages and then it's over with the Resurrection. We won't get to control each other in the afterlife. So, the focus is on this life, a couple helping each other to get God's tasks accomplished.

We work our guts out to pay off mortgages, college, cars, and babies and for what. Remember the rich farmer with plans to build bigger barns. The response to this was, "But God said to him, "Fool! This night your soul is required of you, and the things you have prepared, whose will they be?"

There are some widows and widowers now who have done all the right things. They paid their dues and built great homes and good marriages. A man I know lost his spouse and said to me one day, "I have all this money and it doesn't mean anything to me."

While our minds are still alert and our bodies mobile, there is still time. Ephesians advised us to be "Redeeming the time, because the days are evil." Husbands and wives work best together when they focus on God's goals for them.

There will be no time or place for selfishness. A life of service to others by a man and wife who love each other is a beautiful thing. As God loved his son so we are to have loved our spouses while serving Him.

It's exciting to think of no more old bodies and tears for spouses who may leave us. Get busy getting fitted for those wings and halos!

Broken Dreams

In 1982 Michael Martin Murphy sang, "Doesn't anybody ever stay together anymore? And if love never lasts forever, tell me what's forever for." He says, "Maybe it's me that's gone crazy, cause I can't figure out why; all these lovers keep hurting each other, when good love is so hard to come by." Almost forty years later Michael, things haven't improved. We're still asking the same question.

A fairly recent study found 50% of first marriages, 60% of second, and 73% of third marriages end in divorce. Twenty percent end in 5 years. Was it unrealistic expectations, too much debt too soon, faith differences, too little time to really get to know each other? I know what happened in my parent's case. Every divorce has a story. They usually end with bitter feelings and lots of anger. Us kids just wanted the nightmare to end.

What makes us decide to stay or go? Alcohol, drug issues, abuse, porn addiction, gambling problems, infidelity, uncontrolled spending, wanting it all right now, all of these can be easily understood to be deal breakers. Sometimes you can't live in it anymore or you'll lose your mind. A lot of times you go back and forth when you try to figure out how to survive out there by yourself. It often isn't clean and is never simple. Your dream or vision for it in the beginning often doesn't measure up to reality a few miles down the road. Were you unrealistic or did the partner not do their part to make the dream come true.

Under the best circumstances two totally different people trying to become a smooth functioning team is a challenge. As with a good team of horses, if one decides to go to totally bonkers, the wagon is headed for the ditch. Selfishness will kill a love; serving one another makes a bond not easily broken.

A friend and his children stopped by the house one day. His wife had stashed money, flown the coop, and left the kids with him. Trying to come out of his emotional crater, I told him, "You can't be in love by yourself." He slowly pulled out of his malaise and found someone else. He told me once he'd like a wife like mine who brought me ice tea while we visited. I told him one day that he didn't see the laundry I did or the dishes I washed when she cooked or the beds I made and the floors I swept.

When a couple serves each other, not keeping score, only trying to get it all done so that you might have a little time to talk or just time alone uninterrupted by others, the odds of staying together go way up. When each is more focused on self than partner, the odds of surviving go way down. Love is action. Marriages thrive on love. May you find that person who gives their all to help make your life the dream you imagined.

Now Who's The Smartest

We've noted over the years the differences between men and women. One area that has stood out has been most women's tendency to create and nurture numerous friendships. I jokingly referred to my wife's eight best friends. Rarely does she find a shortage of friends to attend movies or share dinners with. Kenny and Dolly recently recorded a new video and song about old friends.

The gist of it is that we can make new friends, but you can't make old friends. When it's time to circle the wagons, old friends will be there to help women make it through the latest crisis, including serious illness and the loss of a spouse. Old friends step in to help her make it through the dark valley as the woman searches for the light at the end of the tunnel.

Most men have casual friends and acquaintances but are not as likely to devote the time and effort to create close friendships. Women are likely to put things aside to address or devote time to issues involving old friends. Most men find their identity in work and activity. We have good friends, but we often don't or won't take the time to move friends into the best friend category. They are not as likely to call in reinforcements as women are in dealing with difficult situations.

Men are more likely to keep issues private as they try to solve issues by themselves rather than sharing the struggle with another person. Rather than lessening the pressure by sharing the burden, men tend to hold on to the problem which may allow the pressure to build up, possibly attributing to health issues and shorter lives.

What makes women look so wise is their recognition of the real lasting value of friendship when contrasted with material wealth. When women face difficult circumstances they are then able to make emotional withdrawals from the bank of old friendships. Most men may have a number of good friends, some we've had for years, but our friendship storehouse isn't as likely to contain the reserves that women have. We often feel we are just too busy to take the time needed to create or strengthen relationships that could help us make it through hard times.

Women are willing to take the time to create lifelong friendships, but men often take for granted the friendship with their spouses that allow them to turn to them for help in solving problems. Women, too, often say their spouses are their best friends, but they also are wise enough to realize that men are not likely to meet all their emotional needs.

Most men are also wise enough to recognize most women's need for strong female friendships. We know our love and care for our spouses helps put meat and potatoes on the plate. The woman's interactions with her best friends and close relationships can add the seasoning a woman needs to have that well-rounded, truly rich life.

I don't feel threatened by my wife's close friendships and her need for time with her girlfriends. I'm grateful to the ladies for helping make her life richer and fuller. Actually, I take it as a compliment that I have a spouse whose friendship and care are valued by other women.

I knew I had a good one when I found her. I didn't realize what a valuable role she would play in the lives of other people, particularly women. That ultimately makes me look smart. And

my wife can tell you I need all the help I can get in that
department.

Remembering the Fun

I'm not sure who I bought the little barn and stable from Atwood's for, Emmie or me. The horses fit in the stable while the rest of the critters and some fencing fit inside the barn. It makes for a quick cleanup. I can leave them over by the TV in the little living room. When I look at them I think of her. They stand ready for her next visit.

When Emmie and I are in the floor playing with the horses, I remember grade school days in the country outside the cafeteria at lunch. I admired the authentic tractors and motor graders. At home I played with bridge nails, blocks of wood, and a lot of imagination. I don't think I ever asked my folks why I didn't have the really cool toys like the other boys. I guess I knew those would have been luxuries we couldn't afford.

As Emmie and I loaded and emptied the barn, it brought back memories of when the boys were little and consumed with Transformers and He-Man. I got to relive my childhood again, this time with realistic figures improved now with lights and sounds. Emmie gave me an excuse to once again have that farm and barns I missed as a kid except in my imagination.

I'm thinking that children and grandchildren are God's excuse to let us be kids again and get that joy we had when there were no adult worries. They probably already exist, but I've thought several times about creating a summer camp for stressed-out adults who need to temporarily get back in touch with the inner child. Sand boxes, tire swings, swimming holes, merry-go-rounds, and any other playground fixtures that might bring out an inner smile when we remember the fun we once had. We might need to take on new identities for the short time we'd be there. In reality, a short stint returning to our childhood would be cheaper than therapy and be a whole lot more fun.

Little kids serve to remind us adults of earlier times, even in our marriages, when we made time for fun. As our adult cares and responsibilities piled up, there often wasn't much time for fun. Married life often evolved into long stretches of a relationship that often barely existed, starved by a lack of fun and attention.

If we've been fortunate to hold our marriages together, then maybe there's time yet to make sure we put a little joy back into our marriages.

We often get so used to daily routines that we just come to accept things as they are. We never get too old for a date night or a short road trip to a diner in a small town nearby. Maybe a handful of flowers or a special dish could brighten up a day for a special person. Sometimes loving actions speak louder than words and often smell or taste better, too.

Healing the Heartache

While living in Germany I had to go to Interlochen, Switzerland for a few days for a conference. It was a sunny but jacket-comfortable day in the shadow of the Bernese Alps and the cool air coming from the not so distant Grindelwald Glacier. I decided to sit outside the coffeehouse on the shore between Lake Thun and Lake Brienz, the source of the name Interlochen, "between lakes."

Far from East Texas I was jotting down a poem about troubled love. Amidst the majesty of glaciers and timeless Swiss Alps I was struggling to come to grips with my small little world and the emptiness you feel when part of your heart is missing. It almost seemed silly in view of such a splendorous backdrop to think that anyone, let alone God, would even have any interest in my personal anguish.

Much like Tantalus in Greek mythology reaching for but not quite able to grasp the object of his desire, I, too, thought I had it about wrapped up. She actually proposed from back in the states. It looked like the end of bachelorhood. Alas, it was not to be. The "C" word had to make an appearance.

Apparently God knew better and spared me. When I left the states the doctor had said benign and she recovered. Ultimately he was wrong. She had become a Christian, so I found peace in that. Later when the ravaging enemy returned to claim her body, I came to understand how God had spared me of a heartbreak that I might not have endured. He knows what we can handle.

We may never know why things work out like they do, but it's reassuring to look back and see how He was moving things for my own good.

Friends who have lost a child carry the pain close to their heart. A friend from Mexico legally in the country told me of the loss of a son he had to leave to die back home. He talked as if it were yesterday. To him, it was. I tried to comfort him by reminding him how he had been blessed with several other children to help ease the pain.

Years ago I stood at the pulpit ten feet from the front pew of First Baptist to try to find consoling words for my friends whose young daughter had just died. I felt like my efforts were feeble. God eventually blessed them with other girls who looked like her to help fill the void in their hearts.

In Switzerland or East Texas, He is there filling the void, putting the plan in motion, looking out for our best, even when the dark clouds make it feel like it is life at its worst.

Cheerios In My Pocket

I am amazed sometimes what I find when I empty my pockets. I'm not brave enough to get my wife to empty her purse. There may be little people living in there. The other evening after keeping Emmie for a while I emptied my pockets and found a Cheerio in my pants pocket. I think I must have picked it up from the floor while putting up her horse barn and stables.

I raised up the roll top and put it inside there with other mementos like the rifle cartridge from my sister's military funeral, a retirement pin, a a name tag from my son's Judge campaign, my other son's College World Series ring, and a mushy note from my wife when I surprised her one day with a spontaneous getaway. I had to resuscitate her after she fainted.

I've heard that you can tell a lot about a person by examining their checkbook/debit card transactions. I think you can tell a lot about a person by checking their pockets or purse. That Cheerio in my pocket reminds me of how on that day Emmie finally ran up to me, grabbed my legs, and wouldn't let go until I picked her up and swung her around in the air for a few revolutions. Until that day my wife totally dominated Emmie's time. I've just kept hanging around looking for the time when she and I could play on the playground at McDonald's or go watch a kid movie at the theater. I never gave up or forced the issue ; sometimes you have to let a kid warm up to you. Good things are worth waiting for.

We've talked a lot over the years about placing too much value on things or the accumulation of material goods, often just to be able to impress others with all our stuff. Then , in the end, the things have no real lasting value to you. We often value the wrong things and fail to cherish the things that have the potential to give us lasting pleasure. I am reminded that an older friend and widower once said to me, "I have all this money, but what good is it doing me." It's doubly frustrating when we finally get all the things we thought would make us happy, only to find too late that we put our money on the wrong horse.

I made it a point early in my career to keep folders in my desk with positive notes and cards from people and I called them called "Positive Things." A year ago I spoke at a friend's funeral. Later that day I got a complimentary text from a friend about my part of the service. I don't save anything much on my phone, maybe a habit I developed of traveling light after 30 years of bachelorhood. Oddly enough, I find myself going to the one message I've saved on my phone and frequently read it for encouragement, not vanity.

I still mow my friend's yard and then visit with my friend's widow on the patio for a while. She serves me refreshments, and I lend her my ear as she continues to struggle with a death too soon. My wife regularly phones, visits, or takes her to dinner. Things usually get a little better for the little widow ladies by the end of the second year. Still, some days are tougher than others.

It's never too early to think about your legacy and what people will think about when they hear or see your name. Maybe you've had the desire to take a peek and listen in at your funeral service just to see what impression you left on people. You can have some effect on that. Early in life is best, but better late than never, figure out what is of lasting importance and let these things guide your life's actions; people will see a clearly defined individual who knows what matters in life, be it a handful of Cheerios or a rifle cartridge from a loved one's military funeral. What we value defines us.

When Much is Given, Much is Required

Luke tells us, "For unto whomsoever much is given, of him shall be much required." Romans says, "Having then gifts differing according to the grace that is given to us." Socrates tells us, "Know thyself." So, if we know ourselves and understand our gifts, then what? The "so what" is a bit scary – much is required.

Whether it's ignorance of scripture or convenient amnesia, we often choose to ignore the second half of that gifts statement. Who wants to go around constantly looking for opportunities to serve and give away our time, talent, and energy to others?

At the end of the day, every one of us is rich. Compared to other times in history and compared to the rest of the world, we're downright millionaires. And even if we have worked hard our entire lives, the truth is that our wealth is a gift. It's a blessing that we haven't worked hard enough to earn. But we forget where it all came from, and we ignore our duty to be generous with that gift.

Today people seem to have a problem with expressing gratitude and thanking people, much less feeling obligated to do something constructive with the wealth they have accumulated.

I was surprised the other day to hear a lottery winner praising God and saying what good things they were going to be able to do for the Lord and others. After the glow is gone and reporters leave, will the resolve remain to share that wealth and remember his pledge.

It's not exactly a curse but that responsibility deal kind of puts a damper on things. It can be a headache trying to figure out how to best use the material wealth. Sudden wealth can bring a lot of cockroaches from out of the cabinet.

We should remind ourselves daily that our time, talent, energy, and wealth have only been loaned to us for a short time. Let's put them to good use.

Dirty Work and Clean Character

The boys started working for me on my side business when they were young. I didn't force them or beg them. One day my oldest boy came to a job site where I was drenched in sweat and covered in dust. He was standing in the front seat next to his mother. She later told me he cried because he saw how hard I was working. Each boy joined the business when they were very young.

As they grew older, I told them they were free to work for another business where they could stay clean and dry, or they could keep working for me, getting dirty and sweaty. I did stress that the dirt washed off, and the bigger paycheck from me could help fatten their bank accounts. With their schedule of sports and activities, they figured working for the old man was an all-around better deal than minimum wage in a clean uniform.

Mike Rowe has done a television show about dirty jobs. I think I'm one of the lucky or odd ones who enjoy getting dirty. I like the feeling of working hard and getting sweaty. Especially after wearing a tie all day, it always made me feel good to shake off the day's frustrations with good old uncomplicated gritty work. My mind grew less jumbled up and my load felt lighter. I could look at my work and see the results of my labor. That wasn't particularly true on my day job.

When offered the opportunity for a promotion in another city, I asked my youngest son's opinion. When told we would have to move, he said he wanted to graduate from his high school. I said ok, we'll just keep on mowing. I knew he was asking for some stability. I could have gone for the bigger money and more prestige, but my son helped me see what was important.

I'm glad I took his advice. It helped build a foundation of security that propelled him into a successful legal career.

Friends have asked me over the years how I taught my sons to be such good workers. My sister even sent me her son to train. I gave him some pointers for a couple of weeks. I think part of the kids' training was watching me work. I worked on projects as if each one were my own. You teach by example.

An unexpected blessing for me was getting to spend quality hours with my sons. I would gladly do it all again to share in their lives whether watching ballgames or mowing together. Dirty jobs become clean money. Sweat equity and elbow grease develop character, clean character. Laziness develops character but not the kind we need. Which way do we want them to go?

Helpmate

She spent the Mother's Day afternoon visiting her mother's grave with her father and then spent time with two older ladies she feels close to. I cooked supper and washed the dishes while she made another run to a nearby neighbor and friend whose husband recently passed within a short time of her mother's passing.

The Bible describes her as a helpmate, but the truth is I think we could both be called that. As long as I remember we have worked together to get it done. In recent years with both of us in retirement I do a big part of the bed making, laundry, cooking, floors, dishes and whatever else since she often subs at her former school to finish up her Social Security. My small side business is easier to handle now than the old long days working after dark sometimes missing kids' bedtimes but not their ballgames.

She ran a daycare from our home keeping all her teacher buddies' kids. She finally gave in and became an official teacher after years of practice at home.

It's hard to imagine a house where one person works all day in or out of the home while the other comes home and plops down in the recliner. Then the partner starts her household chores. We figured out earlier that if both of us were carrying the load, we could get done sooner and then both could rest for a little while. It had nothing to do with women's lib and more about fairness in a relationship. My mom used to help my dad pick cotton when I was little.

On the farm we worked till it was all done. In truth I reckon that a lot of durable marriages that weathered the storms were probably based on some sort of fairness. Alabama used to sing a song called "It Works" where dad rattled his glass and mom brought a refill. That sounds unfair until we find that dad probably did a lot of things out of sight to help earn that tea glass privilege. A friend whose wife left him saw my wife doing something nice for me like that. He liked that. I told him that she and I had built a mutual admiration society based on fairness and serving one another. It was too late to save his marriage, but I hoped it might help him later.

Over the years my wife did any number of kindnesses for my co-workers during holidays and special weeks. She kept me up on birthdays, anniversaries, etc. and generally made me look good as they felt appreciated, probably the easiest thing to do and often the most neglected in the workplace. We rarely had any employee leave our school and had a waiting list of prospective employees.

One boss asked me if I stockpiled applicants. I tell people I retired and the world went on. However, they cried when they realized my wife wasn't going to be there for them. I couldn't have done it without my helpmate. I always tell people she's the nice one in the marriage.

Plowing a Straight Row

As a young boy, I watched my dad plow a straight row with Jim and Coalie. Soon I tried my hand with our little Ford tractor. One day I asked the secret of keeping the rows straight. I was told to pick a target at the end of the field and stay focused. It worked.

My oldest son is a consultant on the California coast in San Diego/La Jolla. His work involves helping people who have reached road blocks in their pursuit of career goals and objectives. He tries to sort through issues that have dammed up people's mental processes and are keeping them from completing projects.

While finishing my doctorate years ago I discovered that thousands of administrators have acquired a title called A.B.D. - All But Dissertation. For various reasons, they will likely spend the rest of their lives with the knowledge that they failed to complete the one project standing in the way of their doctorate.

A 94 year old veteran finally received his degree after a 76 year gap of time. There is a world of people out there unlike this veteran who have yet to finish a particular goal or project. My wife took 15 years off to raise a family before going back to college in her 30's. Many people live with the regret of not getting their GED or college degree. They usually find that without diplomas and degrees, rising through the ranks of an organization becomes more difficult or nearly impossible. Completing educational goals doesn't necessarily make you a better person, but they do show a level of determination required to complete a task.

Many people live for years or even lifetimes trying to get up the gumption to start a new career, to go out on their own, to step out on faith and make their dreams a reality. What is often missing is a lack of focus on the objective. If a person loses their direction or gets distracted, they cannot complete the task.

To be successful a person must be able to picture a completed task, a finished product. The laser focus can only come from within the individual. People like my son may help jar loose something to get the ball rolling again, but without a person's total focus and dedication no goal can be reached.

In Luke we are asked, "For which of you, intending to building a tower, sitteth not down first, and counteth the cost, whether he has sufficient to finish it?" If it itches, do you scratch it? You do if you are totally committed to it and can look all the way to the end of the row and see your target. You may have to eat the elephant a bite at a time, but if you are hungry enough, get to chewing.

A Lasting Gift

Christmas is almost here. I know because the Hallmark Channel has been running holiday movies 24 hours a day since before Thanksgiving. Some nights we've been lucky to have a fire in the fireplace when the daily temperature wasn't sneaking back up to 70 degrees. Our tree went up the day after turkey day. The Christmas pretties have replaced the pumpkins and harvest scenes, while the outside lights are twinkling. The apple juice in the fridge is ready to mix it up with a handful of red hots to make that steamy delight that blows up my blood sugar level each year. Oh to be young again when all I worried about was my complexion.

This year Emmie's almost two. At our house Christmas Eve she'll practice shredding wrapping paper getting ready for the big day tomorrow. The wife and I will open the handful of things we've asked each other for early Christmas morning and then head out to the country to see the granddaughter destroy more paper on the wrapped ones at her house that weren't brought by Santa.

Then Mamaw and Papaw can head on down the road for a little day trip while Emmie is off to the other grandparents for another frenzy of paper ripping and grandparent spoiling. She'll probably enjoy the paper and empty boxes most of all. She likes to sit in a big box and watch Peppa Pig on her tablet. A kid has to get dizzy opening all these goodies and making time to momentarily appear to enjoy each toy. Could they end up suffering from toy burnout. I once proposed with ours that we put up half of them and bring them back out around July when they had become bored with the first batch. I quickly got voted down on that one.

Far away many centuries ago in a little hilly place another child entered the world and grew up in a quieter, humbler quarters. His path, a rugged one, would be as tough as the Judean hills surrounding the area. He wouldn't grow up experiencing the excesses we all like to heap on our children and grandkids these days. They had their holidays, but probably nothing compared to our modern ritual of December 25.

Life would have been pretty basic for a poor carpenter with a growing family. Had some tradition like Christmas existed for the Jewish family then, it might have looked like some of ours long ago with maybe only gifts of fruit or a single gift, if even that being exchanged. You and I know that stuff doesn't make us happy, especially if it takes us until July to pay it off. I think a lot of us remember our simpler beginnings on a farm or in a small town. Unlike our children and grandkids who may have felt overwhelmed as they sat in the midst of a sea of toys and gadgets, we were able to totally focus on and genuinely appreciate the small gifts we got back then.

Whether it is our desire to give our offspring what we didn't have then or simply us grandparents doing what we do best, spoiling grandkids, we're probably helping the young ones to have to deal with the flood of goodies they get this time of year. Hopefully none of us adults will forget that what they want most is a home, any size, filled with love and the knowledge that family and supporters will always be there to love them. Stuff is nice, but a kid will pick love first every time.

For us old timers and that young one growing up in a big family by a carpenter's shop far away, nobody had to remind us what mattered. For many of us, life was pretty simple. What little we got, we knew what sacrifice had been made to give us that gift. Likewise, today, believers are reminded of the gift we've been given and the great sacrifice that far outshines anything created by or given by human hands.

Hard To Be Cocky

Mac Davis used to sing a song "Oh Lord it's hard to be humble when you're perfect in every way." He brags about his tight blue jeans. Heck, all I want is a pair of relaxed fit; I even started wearing my shirt out like they do in Hawaii. I might even consider cutting a couple of slits in the waistband when I grow to that in between size that's a little too snug. That might let me save a buck before I grow into that even numbered size.. The problem is if I did that and then lost a little weight, you could get arrested for injury to someone's eyeballs if gravity took over and tugged at my drawers.

We survived and actually enjoyed hosting our two separate family Thanksgiving lunch and dinner. The night crew were a little younger and got a little rowdy with that game where you keep turning this little handle until you turn it the designated number of times or until a scoop of whipped cream smacks you in the face. It's a gut buster until it's your turn in the barrel, as they say. When the crowd left and cleanup was about done, I was in the bedroom/computer room lying in the floor on my back shoving a folding table under the bed.

As I lay there like a turtle upended on his shell, my wife offered assistance to help me up. I told her just to get me a pillow; I kinda liked it down there. Besides, I didn't want to further injure her aching back as a result of days of cooking and cleaning for Thanksgiving. In addition, it might take me a few minutes to figure out how to get into position to get up without putting weight on the bad knee. Now which one is it? She and I are a pair. Ok, just get me up and get me headed in the right direction and I'm good.

You're walking along thinking all is well when the twinge in your left hip says, "Not." I think that's God's way of keeping us humble. You get a little cocky and out of nowhere a new ache humbles you momentarily. A cute girl walks by and winks; you figure she just got some dirt in her eye; however, you hear a ding on your phone and think she magically texted you, only to realize it's your pharmacy letting you know your incontinency prescription is ready for pickup.

At this stage of your life you better have developed a good sense of humor. We often do or don't do a ton of things each day that could complete the checklist that would qualify us for "the home." You better laugh or you'll cry. Hopefully nobody's looking when we pull a funny. Ever left a perfectly good Bible or a good pair of shoes on the roof of your work truck as you rushed into a bathroom to change into work clothes and then driven off?

Fortunately a neighbor found and returned the Bible. Its cover has "JAH" in whiteout on it; My wife hates it , but nobody at church would ever claim it. Regarding my good school shoes, I was driving down the street soon thereafter in my yellow El Camino and looked up to see a homeless guy walking along in my shoes giving me a thumbs up. I wonder how he recognized me. He was pointing to my old shoes and grinning. See, God does have a sense of of humor, and that guy has a nice pair of footwear. Oh well, at least I can finally think of something to tell her I need for Christmas.

Small Town

My father-in-law and I started eating a quail dinner at a local BBQ place every Wednesday evening after his wife died last year. Getting used to eating by yourself after 62 years of togetherness can be pretty tough. I was under the weather one Wednesday, so the next week the owner of the restaurant said they had called the law to search for us. They missed us. Such is life in a small town.

The local lawn mower shop keeps our business rolling. I've often told them how much they have contributed to our successful operation. I always buy all my equipment from them; they fix it quickly because they know people are counting on me. Friends help out in a small town.

We go to my father-in-law's favorite Mexican restaurant on Mondays. He and his wife used to eat there faithfully on that day. Also, his favorite waiter works on that night; they give each other a hard time all in good fun. It also doesn't hurt that the owner works that night, too. He comes and sits at our table where my father-in-law likes to wave the bill in front of him several times during conversation to see if he can get him to comp a free meal.

It actually works pretty often. I kinda like the place, too. Many years ago they created a special plate for my staff Christmas dinners that I hosted each year. They named it the Juan Special. Some time later they added it to the menu and called it something else. A group of my old staff members had me join them again recently and order up our old special. Relationships matter in a small town.

An old neighbor a couple of streets away overdoes it on his bike riding. Someone sees him stopped. Soon they've got him loaded up, got the family called, and they get him home to make sure he's ok. They knew who to call and where to reach them. It happened in a small town.

Two friends and fellow church members on the way to church early one Sunday morning arrive at the same time upon a local policeman in a deadly wrestling match as a bad guy is struggling to get control of his service revolver. One guy squats down on the bad guy's legs, the other grabs the arm reaching for the gun, and the officer takes the other arm. Soon the criminal is cuffed, and the drugs are retrieved from beneath a squad car that has just arrived. The slightly wrinkled friends continue on their way to church. Another day in a small town.

A young man flags someone down in the darkness coming into our neighborhood. He starts work tomorrow on a new job, but tonight he says the police make him park his car for no insurance. He has no money. He wants to move the car down the service road to his apt. A strong rope and a short tow gets it safely back home. A little act of kindness in a small town.

My son successfully runs for office. An acquaintance offers the use of his billboard downtown for a few months. Mama and I happily get to see baby Emmie and parents in a Texas-size picture. For the next few months our car just seems to gravitate over that way when we are in town, no vanity or pride here. It's a little excitement for some old folks in a small town.

Large cities have a lot to offer, but I went around the world and chose or God allowed me to settle back home in my hometown. We don't have everything, but we have caring people. Every day people here and in hometowns across the country take the time to help a cop or a stranger for no other reason than kindness. All these actions put together make a place you proudly call your hometown, and you wouldn't want to live anywhere else. Home sweet home is not just a slogan.

Change

Back in the 1970's Alvin Toffler's book <u>Future Shock</u> said the greatest challenge we will face as we get older would be the rapidity of change. Who could have guessed the impact of computers on all facets of our daily existence. For most of us older folks it seems we fight a losing battle against the constant way technology keeps affecting our lives. Whether it is the HD TV or the car radio, nothing is getting simpler.

At times you want to scream. An old friend called the other night because he got all set to watch his favorite western rerun only to find that it was being broadcast in another language. The company tried to fix it over the phone, but the last I heard they were bringing in more help. Any wonder we're starting to have small shiny spots on our scalps.

Our phones deserve their own special section. For much of the world's population the phone has become like a third hand. It is almost an attachment to our bodies. I used to notice the imprint on a guy's rear jeans pockets made by their Skoal snuff can. Now, especially girls, the phone is jammed into the rear pocket. If my wife says she caught me looking at a girl's rear pocket, I really was just looking at her phone.

As a young married guy I had a summer job repairing and replacing upholstery, especially bar stools, because they were harder for me to mess up. In a café one night with my wife, I found myself looking at a bar stool at the counter. I really was checking out the workmanship and stitching, not noticing the attractive blond girl sitting on it next to a big guy I used to see on the Popeye cartoons. Looking up I saw a big ugly look from a jealous man. I think we made a hasty exit as my wife complained about not getting to finish her pie.

Identity theft continues to be a problem as criminals continue to hack our accounts through our computers and phones, including Facebook. I have had two replacement or updated credit cards stolen from the mail on their way to me before I ever received them. Some guy in Louisiana got some high dollar tennis shoes on me. Recently someone in Kentucky got a $500 visit to a spa on me. Heck, it hurts me to pay $15 for a basic haircut.

We don't even get the good smellum stuff splashed on our neck. Like I said, things are really changing, not necessarily for our own good. Shoot, the scammers are now calling you with local numbers showing up on caller ID. Twice they have used numbers of people I know. I called them back to tell them that scammers were using their local number to fool us on the other end as we looked at our phones. I will brag on the credit card companies for reimbursing my accounts each time I had an illegal charge on a card.

It's hard not to be in a constant state of anxiety and frustration as traffic gets rerouted for construction or lights go into flashing mode at intersections and our aging brains have to be careful not to get confused and pull out at the wrong time. I think we begin to lose a little of our self-confidence as we start second guessing ourselves about distances, especially at night.

We try to keep up a brave front, but more and more a lot of us don't like to face the prospects of driving toward bigger cities on the roads as the amount of traffic, especially trucks, increases. How about getting through the airport lines or paying

139

in a restaurant at your table on the little computer terminal, or the self- checkout line at the big box stores. We lose contact with humans and have to battle machines.

The young ones laugh at us old guys as banks, hospitals, and just about everyone else is trying to force us to do everything by computer rather than having to pay humans to talk to us. Many of us just want to find a good ole mom and pop country store and café and reminisce about the good old days. All I say to us older guys is don't go aggravating the younger ones, or as the Bible says, "Frustrate not your children." Throw in grandkids, too.

Now how did they know way back then that we were going to need someone to set up our remotes and program those big TV's for us. My only consolation is what goes around comes around. Someday they'll be the ones looking for their teeth or the glasses on their heads. That's not much comfort but it helps.

Waiting On Jack

Called my youngest son, an expectant father, a little while back and asked how things were going. He simply said, "We're waiting on Jack." As of this writing, Jack was scheduled to make an appearance the following week. Not sure Jack has gotten the word. Clay felt like it would be sooner rather than later. For the women's benefit, she's at a "3" right now. So who knows.

I doubt that Jack, named after Christian writer C.S. Lewis, has any clue about his fan club who have eagerly awaited his arrival for nine months. Most likely he'll raise a fuss about being pulled out of a soft, warm cocoon of water into the glare of delivery room lights and noises that hurt his sensitive ears. Soon enough he'll be wrapped up in a warm blanket and laid onto his mother's soft chest just above a beating heart he's faintly heard for so long through his muffled surroundings.

As Jack listens, he hears familiar sounds, both male and female. He's comforted by the gentleness of the words and softness of their caresses. The old watery home was great, but maybe the new, drier place won't be so bad. People keep scrubbing and wiping and wrapping and unwrapping him. They're putting things on his head and dodads on his wrist. Rude people have been staring at him through a glass into a room full of other little guys. Jack is getting ready to blow this place.

Sure nuff, Jack gets his wish. Soon he's moving on some sort of magic carpet as a low hum vibrates beneath his carrying case. Eventually it stops, and he feels cool air on his face as he once again is in the light, this time not as harsh as before. In the driveway Jack is greeted by other strange creatures with unfamiliar sounds and too many legs. The caravan trudges on to another place out of the bright sunlight and into a place with space to spread out and warm covers to seal off the cool air.

As Mommy holds him close, he satisfies his need for nourishment and security. A soft voice repeats the promises and dreams he's heard before through the watery incubator. A deeper voice he also recognizes reassures him of being loved and wanted. The memory of life in Mommy's tummy is already fading as the sweetness of the warm liquid on his lips and the salty liquid from her eyes replace a world of abstract sounds without form.

As Jack makes his home in his new sleeping quarters, the four-legged creatures check out the new arrival. The toddler also gathers round to look at the new arrival. The cat coolly sniffs at the bundled form while the dog instinctively moves sideways up against Jack's bed as if to tell admirers they've come close enough. He's in charge of security here.

Last but not least, baby Emmie, no longer the baby and now sharing her star power with the new arrival, sidles up to Mommy and Jack; she looks up with concern in her eyes and puzzlement on the corners of her mouth. The eyes of baby Jack seem to momentarily focus on toddler Emmie's questioning eyes as if to say, "I know you, too. I've heard your sounds and words before. It will be okay. I'm here now. Never fear. Gus will protect us. Mommy and Daddy have got this. No more waiting on Jack. Move over Big Sister."

Morning

It's morning. One more morning He gave me. I embrace it because I know that from the day I was born the calendar was set. Each day is a designated gift with a special blessing. They are finite in number. God gave us our allotted days and said, "Use them wisely." I open the blinds as the brilliant sun pours into the room. It's a clear and cold day. Not too many of these in East Texas. I'll remember it in July as I retreat to the shade of a large live oak.

As I sit down in front of the fire with something warm to sip on and get me started, I feel the warmth on my back. Another day. What a gift. Last night Emmie came to see me and danced in front of the tv for me. You can't buy entertainment like that anymore, especially from a Shirley Temple clone. Naturally she pulled me away from my football game with her two year old hand signals telling me I have to come do "the wheels on the bus go round and round" with her, complete with choreography. Maybe God created little ones to get us up and moving more than we had planned. They don't take excuses. Do this and gimme that. He knew we needed to get the tugboat out of dry dock and into the water.

Jack came to see me, too. We couldn't see each other, but he could hear me. I could feel him as he kicked against his mommy's tummy ready to "break outta da joint." Everybody agrees it's time except the Great Timekeeper. In reality, as Christ existed before He came to earth and made his appearance, so, too, Jack's timeclock has been ticking for months before he makes his grand entrance. Something so tiny occupying so much of our thoughts and prayers as we long for a safe passage on his way to his new home. Who knew yesterday morning as the sun hid itself on a dreary looking day that I'd be blessed before the day was over with smiles and giggles no rich man could buy at any price. It was a bonus in the gift of another day.

Funny how our days dissolve and disappear, even as we watch the clock . Make the bed—why, I'm just gonna crawl back into it in a few hours. Run a load of laundry—usually small. Wash a couple of my breakfast dishes at the sink if I didn't forget to save my Whataburger cup and my Braum's plastic spoon so that I didn't have to wash anything. Not much need for the dishwasher these days. I like the time of standing in front of the sink and looking out the kitchen window. It gives me time to think and reflect. We do a lot more reflecting now instead of doing. Did I meaningfully redeem my days? Hope so.

In the former days of hustle and bustle with too much work, too little pay, too little time for yourself and now—it's time to think, time for self. Time for phone calls and texts with family and friends. The beep and the ding or whistle on the cell phone tells you someone's checking on you. You can't buy that; maybe you wish you could. Before you know it, it's noon and then evening. Where did the time go? You wondered at sunrise what you'd do with a bonus of twenty four hours more. You outlasted the rich farmer in the Bible who passed in the night never getting to build those bigger barns.

Already you're a winner. Maybe tonight before you lay your head on your pillow again, you'll be lucky enough to get a visit from little urchins who pull you out of your chair to dance. If

144

not, get up and do it anyway. People may already think we're a little off. What does one more little jig by yourself hurt.

In Front Of Our Eyes

Used to we didn't talk about it. You got the bruise or scratch or broken arm when you tripped or fell down the stairs. Mama wouldn't tell, and the kids were afraid to say anything.

Wished we could say things had gotten better, but I don't think so. Read the police/sheriff reports in the local paper. The dope and alcohol just stir up the do-do. Real people with real kids are paying the price. Little children are coming to school with suspicious bruises and circular burns.

One child told me how they followed the mother from place to place each night just hoping to have a recliner to sleep in. We often fed the child at 9-10 in the morning if they made it to school at all. Sometimes we would go pick the student up if they were at home. Others I had to pull out from under beds skipping school while mama's boyfriend was sleeping in the living room.

There's nothing like visiting a family of kids' home with empty pantry, windows broken out, water being run unknowingly from the neighbor's faucet, and the filthy clothes they wore came from the pile in the floor. Their food came from school. We washed their clothes at school and found other clothes to wear from the lost and found. Those I was able to get into foster care with the help of a judge.

Others fled before CPS could get a handle. For my last 25 years as a principal I solved problems. Sometimes with the help of some good advice and able assistance, we made a difference. Unfortunately, sometimes nothing seemed to help.

You ask yourself why a kid goes bonkers and shoots up a school or shoots at a bus out in the country. Ephesians says, "And you fathers, provoke not your children to wrath: but bring them up in the nurture and admonition of the Lord." When the family is screwed up and exasperation leads to anger, what does a kid do with the pending explosion.

As a consultant my son has worked on that issue of unresolved frustration and anxiety as people struggle to get a handle on their thoughts and process them in an orderly fashion. Fortunately most people don't resort to violence on the grand scale to vent a lifetime of frustration. The problem is that kids tossed to and fro can become damaged and lost. Some become desensitized to feelings, good or bad.

Schools are scrambling now to try to put in place metal detectors and mental detector programs to be proactive in identifying red flags warning of potential human time bombs. We look for bullying. We often overlook threats on social media. Oh for the good old days when we followed up on rumors and got to wrestle away a gun from a middle school football player when I was coaching.

Guns don't kill. People pulling triggers do. In England with no guns available they use knives. In the Middle East as long as I can remember they've used car bombs to wreak havoc. We missed one by a hair the day I left the Golan Heights of Israel/Syria. If all we had were clubs, and that once existed, then killers would be Alley Oop and use clubs.

The more unstable our families and life in general become, prepare for the worst. In the end times the Devil will increase his activity as his time is short. For believers it's happening before our eyes.

Miracles and Mysteries

I was looking in my flower beds one day at the cockscombs or prince feathers I had dug up out of a neighbor's pasture and transplanted at home. Next to it were some Mexican petunias I "borrowed" from a lady's bed to get a start. Those bluish/purple flowers dominate now.

My wife and I argue about the color. Lighting on one was my little buddy up from Mexico, a monarch butterfly. It's July here as I write this, so it's time for them to come back from the amazing migration from Canada to Mexico and back. As they lay eggs it takes about four generations for them to make their annual cycle. That's a lot of butterfly eggs.

As you get an opportunity to think about it, imagine the miracle of it all. How do they know how and when to migrate? How do geese and whooping cranes know when to travel? Unbelief is hard work. Believers can open their eyes and be amazed. On the Canadian border I dipped out rainbow smelt as they migrated like lemmings in the icy cold streams; I fried them whole like crunchy French fries. Buzzards routinely return to Hinkley, Ohio, and swallows do the same to Capistrano in California during March.

How do they know? Have you ever watched the bonding of mothers and babies? Where does that instinct come from? How are babies and other newborns provided medicine in the form of colostrum to help them fight off infection as a newborn? Who came up with that? Does it boggle your mind to think about how many miracles and mysteries we just routinely take for granted without a second thought.

Talk about faith or lack of it, take a minute to take inventory. Feel your pulse and wait for the next surge of blood. Put your hand over your heart and feel the next heartbeat. Put your hand on mommy's tummy as you feel that little foot kick for the first time. All of this we take for granted. Remember the farmer in the Bible who God called a fool as he planned for bigger barns.

"This very night, thy soul shall be required of thee." I watched the I Tune video seen by 50 million followers of DonnaTaggert the Irish Celtic singer singing the Jenn Bostic song, "Jealous of the Angels." She sings of the suddenness of departure and the numbness that comes when we come to know that our departed loved ones are not coming back to earth. She is jealous of the other angels who have a new singer gathered around the throne. We put crosses beside the highways and decals on our back windshields in memory of loved ones. We are jealous of the angels.

Today we do not want to live with regrets. Say or show how you feel about someone close to you now. You may not get to say those words you intended. Your barns may not get built. They tell me that what makes God smile is humans making plans.

Survivors

On my return from officer training at Ft. Benjamin Harrison in Indiana, my oldest sister met me at the airport. I was on my way to the Canadian border to my next military assignment. Our job was to protect the northern border from invasion by Russian bombers. Our good old B 52's stood ready to return the favor. Likewise I went half way around the world years later, only to find that our mission there was to chase those pesky Russian Mig jets back across the East German border with our F4 fighter jets. They mostly just messed with us to see how much they could get away with.

My plans were momentarily delayed as my sister drove me to the hospital to see my mother. My last of 4 sisters was a teenager at home. My mother had had the chance to remarry and live comfortably, never sewing another stitch on a pair of HD Lee blue jeans as she had for years. Uneasy over the prospective living arrangement, including a grown son of his at home while her teenage daughter was still at home caused her to pause and finally decide to forego the marriage proposal.

Soon after dating my mother for two years, he hastily married another lady in a matter of months, as some widowers are more likely to do than widows. Whether it was regret, because he was a nice man, or the prospect of her last child leaving home in a few short years, thus leaving her alone, who knows. Sleeplessness set in followed by medication and depression led to an overdose meant to kill, not just as a cry for help. My little sister found her, got a neighbor to get the ambulance. She was saved and never tried it again.

Unless you have battled depression, it's hard to understand how debilitating it can be. Look at Marilyn Monroe as she checked out of her marriage to Arthur Miller and was memorialized in the song by Elton John, "Candle In The Wind." He revamped the song again upon the death of Princess Di, another beauty who also died a tragic death as she searched for true love while literally giving up the kingdom.

Other families haven't been as fortunate as ours. Many have found family members only moments too late. Some have chosen carbon monoxide, gun shots, and deliberately running their cars into object with a true death wish. Some slit wrists while others took a little longer like a fellow teacher and one of my favorite country singers, Keith Whitley, as they let the whisky do the deed. When Keith sang, "I'm No Stranger to the Rain", he was a rising star married to another gorgeous country girl, Lorrie Morgan. That's hard to comprehend. On a lighter but equally insane note, what about the crazy fool who gave up his beautiful cheerleader from a pro sports team so that he could have more time to play more video games. As Larry the Cable Guy would say, "Lord, that ain't right."

My boyhood friend and fellow baseball team member finally gave in to the pressure of his totally draining occupation as counselor to people struggling to right their ships on the way to prison. The quiet, dependable strong warrior seemingly had the American dream but couldn't see that even heroes need a little R&R. He chose to let his family find the rope.

Anyone cheated by this act can tell you what a cruel trail suicide leaves behind. The deceased may have finally escaped some personal Hell caused by bullying, bad financial choices, fear of embarrassment, the list goes on. Remember grown men jumping out skyscrapers in 1929 when Wall Street fell in New York. What's left behind are usually more questions than answers. The burden of guilt seems to fall on everyone who has contact with the victim. What ifs and if onlies keep surfacing. I've seen family members blame another for years; they were convinced that one spouse had driven the victim to it when it was obvious the deceased had left a long trail of bad choices. The family would gladly have bailed the person out one more time, but another land mine was waiting for the next bad move.

It seems that depression as in my mother's case ultimately turned her into a person too weak to fight the battle of the mind. The victims often become people we hardly recognize with little willpower and only desiring to get out from under an unbearable burden.

Spouses blame self. Kids often blame the "surviving" parent. If divorce is a living death, suicide is a living hell for those left behind. You keep thinking how someone would rather leave you than stay here and fight the battle. It seems so selfish in a way. How is a spouse supposed to feel about themselves when their partner couldn't make them want to stay more than they wanted to leave. It's not that simple, but it will blow the hell out of a surviving spouse's self-esteem. Some never recover to love again.

Others are blessed to find peace or a loving heart to help them love again. In my mother's case not only was there guilt but also the anxiety of when she might try it again. That didn't help my situation as I headed overseas shortly afterwards. There isn't a lot of room for divided minds in the military. A common phrase we often heard was , "He who hesitates is dead" Ask any good policeman. Guilt and fear of a repeat attempt can follow you around the world and stir up a big pot of anxiety.

Family members and friends of victims go on with their lives knowing all the while that something is missing. John Donne said that each person's death diminishes us. Since each one of us is made in a unique fashion with a special role to play while we are here, we move on, knowing we are one person short on our journey.

Moving On

The other day I heard Vince Gill singing about regret. It got me to thinking about how much time we waste looking back on things we can't change. If we were able to learn something from it and not repeat it, then a little self-examination is a good thing. Some people spend way too much time looking back and not looking forward. In Christian terms we say that the Devil knows he can't take our salvation, but he constantly works to take our joy and make us a defeated person whose life wouldn't draw anyone to ask us the key to our happiness and peace.

We all have things we wish we could have done differently. At the time in the frame of mind and circumstances we were in, we're now looking back on it through the eyes of experience and maturity. A teen or young adult confronted with what to do about a life-changing issue might not think about the future; they just want out of a bad situation. Those actions can set in motion events that can haunt you the rest of your life. Later as you lie awake at 3 in the morning in the midst of a good life you've built, the what ifs may try to creep back in and rob you of precious sleep.

This is when forgiveness kicks in. We need to ask forgiveness and forgive ourselves. What's done is done. David and Bathsheba messed up, but God still loved the man after his own heart. David didn't get to build the Temple, and Moses didn't get to enter the Promised Land. Sampson still did not get back his sight. God forgave the heroin addicts we were able to reach in Germany, but they didn't get new livers. God could do that, but we still usually pay a price for our decisions. Sin pays more than any of us ever imagined, but grace overlooks that.

155

What we do with the rest of our lives is up to us. Ask the woman at the well who faced discrimination as a hated Samaritan in a Jewish world. He simply told her to go and sin no more. Peter, the only normal guy I know of who had enough faith to walk on water, turned around and denied knowing his best friend.

I would say good riddance to a guy like that. I never trusted a car battery or soldier that let me down in a crunch. I might love them; I just couldn't trust them again. As a policeman or in the military the cost could be everything. Yet, Peter was forgiven and allowed to help build a band of believers numbering in the thousands. Samson got one more surge of power as a final wish as he literally brought down the house.

When we have messed up, we have a choice; face the music, ask forgiveness, and move on or remain stuck in a state of emotional paralysis, sometimes anesthetized with pills or alcohol. It's a lot easier to remain stuck in self-pity and self-defeat than to get off our duffs and take that first step on a journey where we determine to learn a lesson and be a stronger, possibly more understanding and forgiving , person because of it. In life we believe the person who has been there and done that.

We may not have had being a role model in mind, but like it or not you have paid the price, perhaps higher than you ever imagined. You are the go to person now for others as a resource person. You truly become a living Bible. Off the top of my head come to mind several women I know who had bad starts and bad first marriages but through grace and newly found wisdom and strong determination were able to finally have the .marriage and life they could only dream of.

Visiting for my church 40 years ago I had an address in a rough part of town. The name was familiar on the card, but it didn't fit. The man I grew up knowing was a well respected, successful farmer. Since then he had left his family, business, and community , relocating with someone else in a little shotgun house. Both the house and the woman were faded shadows of their better days. I had grown up in a place like this, sans electricity and plumbing. Ironically I would have thought this a castle as a little boy.

On this day it stood as a monument of how high a price a person had better be ready to pay for bad judgment. Gone were the respectability and prosperity. I've often wondered what regrets, what thoughts, he had on looking back. The miles reflected in his eyes. The shell of the man I once lived in awe of for his land and possessions wasn't so intimidating as he briefly visited with me. A spark momentarily came to his eyes when I reminded him of those days of planting and harvest.

The crop he had planted now yielded a bitter harvest. Forgiveness was still within reach; regaining his former life of prosperity was not at this late stage. His surroundings said it all. He seemed to be stuck in the regret stage. I hoped he would be able to overcome it and find peace. The grains of sand were slipping through the hourglass.

Moving Off High Center

I grew up on farms in East Texas with accompanying county roads. Oil roads then were a luxury. Things hadn't changed a lot 20 years later when I got back from the wars looking for a teaching job. The superintendent at my country alma mater offered me a job and threw in a sundae with a cherry on top—a school bus driving job for extra pay on a, get this, oil top road. Good to know some things still have value. I hadn't felt that important since I left the farm the summer before my 6th grade year.

A client agreed to buy a policy from my father in his new business if he agreed to to let me play on his ball team since the team draft was over. Talk about pressure to perform. I think I was hired to chase down balls that the first baseman missed, which were many. Yes I did wilt in the 100 degree heat after about the zillionth wild throw. The good thing is I fell in love with a 5th grader named Elizabeth who daubed my brow on a couch across from the ballfield. Had I known she would be head twirler in the gold lame sparkling outfit years later, I might have tried to fake an injury or something to at least impress her a little. That's hard when you look like a 60 pound version of Casper the Friendly Ghost.

In the country we mostly had slick muddy clay roads in winter and deep sandy roads in summer, each with their own traps. You tried to drive in the ruts, but that also had its own drawbacks. Ruts are good unless they're deeper than the tires. Then you get this country road phenomenon called high center. Four- wheel drive would then be summoned in the form of a team of horses or later a tractor. Good luck not tearing up your under carriage.

In my lifetime I've run across a lot of people seemingly stuck on high center, whether it's a doctoral dissertation undone facing a deadline or an issue of commitment with a relationship going nowhere. Ever had an idea or possible invention in mind only to wait and then see someone come out with it later?

Going back to college, enrolling in nursing school, GED classes, welding classes, switching careers is scary. Years ago I was offered a promotion to a new job in a nearby town. My eldest son was headed out of state to play college baseball. When I asked my youngest high school son about us moving and taking the job, he said he wanted to stay and graduate with his class here. With that I told them thanks but no thanks to the promotion and continued on with our principal/lawn care dual career. His happiness came first; there was no long anguishing battle about what to do. Not all decisions are that clear.

As I was preparing to leave the military for civilian life in Germany, I had job offers to stay in the country and be a supervisor for the motion picture service that supplied movies for all Europe and another to help run my friend's charter airline that furnished flights for all the soldiers in Europe flying to and from America then . Throw in the fact that I could keep my youth director job at my church in my little German town, have a new car, eat great food, and travel all over Europe on their dime made for a couple of great temptations. Throw in an offer for a seven year assignment to teach English at the Air Force Academy with an early promotion to Major, and you have another plum job offer.

That job would pretty well ensure that I knew what I would be doing for a career in the military while my fellow Air Force officers were beginning to line up airline pilot jobs for their families as Viet Nam was winding down. For many of them the term RIF meant they had to find a new line of work. Having gotten used to the pay, lifestyle, and opportunities to travel, civilian life would be a step down from what they were used to. Ultimately as a single guy with no wife to sway me, I took the practical route of returning to Michigan to finish my graduate work and teacher certification that I had started when my giirlfriend's school board president father got me started on while I was based close to their school.

She passed too young. It was hard knowing she wasn't coming back, but travelling to our old haunts there made it almost feel like her spirit was present there. Cancer is no respecter of age or beauty; it's an equal opportunity destroyer. <u>Love Story</u> is not my favorite movie.

My wife was on a fast track in her banking career that she loved when our first born became ill. We had lost our first baby, Jamie Leigh. My wife gave it up to stay home with him. Being a business person like her dad, she started a successful day care. As time went on she began to feel she was meant for a career in Early Childhood Education. After 9 years one day I sneakily and secretly went over to the university and found her an advisor, got her a class schedule, and returned home.

When I asked her if she was ready to starve and go back to school with one less income and a full-time college student at home, she said yes. I said, "Good. Here's your schedule." We had three lean years, but she tells everyone it was the best decision she/we ever made. The hardest part was keeping her in line when she filled in for me at my school during her training. My teachers tried to spoil her.

Sometimes when you're stuck on high center and undecided, you may just need a friendly nudge from someone close to you or just turn a tough situation into an opportunity. Life takes funny bounces sometimes. As in our marriage with its unlikely start at a Ranger ball game, the crooked road that brought us straight to where we are today consisted of a lot of decisions that resulted in something we could never have foreseen. Pick your poison and drink it up. As Forest was fond of saying, "My mom always said life was like a box of chocolates. You never know what you're gonna get."

Available For Service

As an old bachelor until 30 I picked up basic household survival skills along the way. I decided to tackle a sewing project. I headed to the laundry room to get Mamaw's sewing basket. I had to use the needle with the big eye. Sometimes these days I think I need the one the camel could go through in the Bible.

As I was looking at her sewing basket, it dawned on me it was the only thing I remember us getting from her estate, at least the thing we made the most use of. Mamaw lived an interesting life in West Texas and became a turned on Christian her last nine years as she battled breast cancer. She chose to forego treatment, having seen her friends endure the rigors of surgery, radiation, and chemo and often not have great quality of life.

It was a very personal choice; she did have nine quality years remaining strong to the end. We went to the nursing home the day before she passed and found her bed made up and the room empty. We thought they may not have called us to tell us she had passed. Not to be, for to no one's surprise at the home, they said she's down in the cafeteria spreading the gospel.

If we all could only go out that way. My wife flew out to Amarillo nine years earlier with two little ones in tow to help her relocate and get settled here. Mamaw came to be a big part of our family. She prayed over my youngest son's health issue, and immediately it stopped. She later prayed over a problem with one of his ears where the tube lodged sideways causing infection and earache instead of helping ease the problem.

As they wheeled him into surgery to fix the problem, the surgeon took one more look at the issue. To his amazement the abnormality was healed. No surgery was needed. Where was Mamaw when my gall bladder gave out.

Mamaw placed her hands on the heads of both of my sons and said that God would bless them. We give her part of the credit for the rich full lives both boys have experienced.

Once Mamaw got on track, she packed more living into her final years than most of us do in a lifetime. She epitomized the phrase, "It ain't where you start but where you finish." She started a Christian coffeehouse to rescue lost men down on their luck. Once she arrived in town her new church was never the same. Mamaw preached forgiveness and shunned regret. She saw it as a tool of the Devil to hold people back. She gave him all he wanted for her last nine years here on earth. She was loyal to her pastor and mindful of her responsibility to reach the lost and bring in the sheaves.

My niece at 40 told my wife before she died that she was grateful for the cancer and would go through it again to be able to spend her last days in the arms of her earthly father as he carried her about and know how much he loved her. A good friend who lost the use of his legs in a car accident told me he wouldn't undo a thing. He operated his furniture refinishing business from his wheelchair. Fin's brother was a successful African American businessman. Fin said had he not been injured he probably would have ended up like a lot of his friends.

My youngest son tore his ACL in his knee and had to take a year off from high school sports. He turned it into an opportunity to hold Bible studies for a hundred teens at our house, complete with band and full drum set, much to the chagrin of the neighbors. When I came home that day after working in the lawns, my wife met me at the back door and told me I couldn't come in. I said I'd take my shoes off. She shook her head. She smiled and said, "There's no room in the inn."

Turning lemons into lemonade isn't for the faint hearted. Taking the old nemesis of cancer and using it for motivation as Mamaw did to change her life and make a lasting difference in this world is a beacon of hope for us all. It reminds us that it is never too late to be used for good. Hopefully it won't take something like a car wreck, cancer, or season ending sports injury to help us feel a sense of urgency. That old sewing basket stands ready to remind us of lives made available for service. Ready to add another name to the list?

Horse Apples

I've been to Paris, France several times and always visited the Eifel Tower, Arc de Triomphe, Notre Dame, Louvre, and the Gardens of Versailles. I rode the camels to the pyramids at Giza, Egypt and walked where Christ walked along the shores of the Sea of Galilee. I was impressed by the Acropolis and the Parthenon in Greece, but I think some of my best memories are of Estes Park, CO, my favorite place in the whole world. A neighbor and friend around the corner thinks she may be moving there one day. I've asked her to adopt me and take me with her. I could keep her lawn there for room and board.

The first time we took that old winding road from the Colorado interstate to Estes Park, I tried to imagine anyone getting in and out of there in the winter, but I bet a four-wheel drive can do it with no sweat. The good thing was that it was June and 50 at night. Late one evening we got a bubbling hot pizza reminding me of Texas Tech nights at Little Italy and Tower of Pizza. Why did it taste so good at midnight and make you feel like yuck at 6 a.m.. The kids and us wolfed it down by a gurgling brook. We hadn't gotten settled good until a herd of elk came strolling by with the cutest baby calves dragging up the rear. The light jacket felt good in the cool evening breeze whistling through the valley.

The following morning was roundup time. Time to head 'em up and move 'em out. I hadn't ridden in a while, but I think my wife's word was "never." We found her a horse, much to the displeasure of the man from the glue factory there to pick him up. It was my first experience of seeing a horse with his own oxygen mask. It was probably just the high altitude. Well, my sons and I moved into position to boost my wife up.

Ryan was fixing to be a counselor at a Christian camp at nearby Long's Peak, and Clay was along to check out the accommodations at the Air Force Academy, so helping Mom get mounted would be good practice for both of them. If we had been in Clay's courtroom today, she might be classified as a "hostile" rider. Her not-so-fleet steed didn't appear to be all that excited about it either. Then again they had a little trouble keeping him awake. Probably his nap time. The three of us did finally get her situated in spite of the strange sounds someone was making in the saddle area. Still not sure if it was the horse or her.

I'm proud to say that both mama and the horse both survived the jaunt around the park. The older horse had a little trouble with his transmission, sometimes wanting to go in reverse instead of going forward. I regret to say I can't put my hand on the video which could be used for blackmail purposes. We may not have gotten it back from America's Funniest Videos.

My wife said that when she went to see the performance of Texas in Palo Dura Canyon near Amarillo later, she was not invited to be a part of the equestrians that ride out with the flags. I could tell it was a big letdown to her. I'm not sure how her reputation as a rider reached all the way to Texas, but as the Martian said upon visiting Earth and encountering a thermos jug of hot coffee next to another one beside it full of ice, "How does it know?' An Earthling asked, "What do you mean?" To which the Martian asked again, "How does it know to keep the hot stuff hot and the cold stuff cold." You just have to chalk some things up to being unexplainable.

At least my wife was never thrown off a horse. Can't say the same for me. One time on a three day ride as a kid I made the mistake of letting my rope jerk back and catch my horse in a sensitive spot of the under carriage. I would have jumped, too. That brings back bad memories of military physicals with big ugly nurses without compassion. Anyway, I momentarily saw my short life flash before my eyes. I suspect that my pride was hurt more than my posterior. I managed to miss the cactus but not the horse apples, or as you tenderfeet refer to as horse poop. Add me to the list of things with company and fish that smell after three days.

I don't think you could tell much difference adding the new odor to the caked-on sweat and horse hair clinging to the thighs on my jeans. I hope I can trust you guys to not tell my wife about this. After all I did try to discuss her riding skills with great sensitivity, and my manly pride is pretty fragile these days.

Genuine Riches

Momma and I were sitting in our favorite steak place, Borderline Café, in Powderly the other day. Even the 8 oz. ribeye almost covered the plate. Remember no credit or debit cards, only cash or checks, out of town ones are accepted. Us old people still could not eat it all; had to stick the leftovers in her purse—memories of our honeymoon. No, not that.

After every meal I usually had a homemade roll or slice of pizza to put in her purse and take back to the cabin on Table Rock Lake. Leaving the Ozarks a day early so that we had enough moolah to pay our first month's rent and stock the fridge, she emptied out her purse. It looked like enough crumbs to last us for a week. She knew she had married a weird one by then. Too late she figured out I was also poor.

What is poor? Who is genuinely rich? My millionaire friend before she died with no spouse or children to leave a legacy to, told me that I was rich. That was news to my wife. I think I laughed at the time, but now I understand what she was really saying. At this writing #4 grandchild is almost here. The new Judge will get his boy to go with the sweetest girl who is our standing Friday night date with a two year old. It only costs us a free meal for the kids. I'd say that was a bargain.

As the wife and I were still stuffing our faces while yet saying how full we were, I asked her for the millionth time, "Ever think about how blessed we are?" Happy kids, healthy grandbabies, no bill collectors calling lately, only the stupid calls from the robot at a credit card company, making our stomach jump while telling us there's no problem; they're just calling us to let us save a lot of money.

I think I tasted the blood as I bite my tongue and put my nonBaptist unspoken thoughts back into my brain. As I grit my teeth I gladly punch Option 2 to take me off the call list. I thought I had already done this twice before.

I know I've done nothing to not have our family touched so far by many of the tragedies like losing children you've come to love or enduring someone's drug rehab or incarceration. It is all purely grace. I know I'm undeserving, no better, no worse, no more important than the next guy. I almost laugh at the big guys who go on about what all they've done, what all they've accumulated.

Hey, let me introduce you to Mr. Farmer in the Bible who passed away during the night as he was drawing up blueprints in his dreams preparing to start building those bigger barns the next morning. What makes God smile is people making plans. Apparently God knows us best and understands who would totally blow it if given a big influx of sudden wealth. I appreciate His thoughtfulness. As my eldest son on the California Golden Coast jokingly told me the other day, he said he had a brief conversation with God.

It went something like this, "Okay God, I understand you have felt the need to help teach me lessons of faith as I endure some tough challenges and lean on you. Now I appreciate what you've helped me learn, but if you wouldn't mind it, I could use a little bit more prosperity." As of this writing the jury is still out. Hope the verdict comes back in favor of the plantiff. Sure don't want to aggravate the JUDGE.

Eating The Elephant

Remember the time Ritchie Cunningham of <u>Happy Days</u> came home tipsy. When quizzed by his dad about how big the beer glass was, he indicated a tiny little jigger. When pressed by his father how many tiny little drinks he had, he replied, "Fifty two." Sip, sip, sip.

I'm not a snack guy in general, particularly sweets, but anything with salt or homemade bread will do.

A little Amish lady in Paris, Texas has some of the best bread and pastries in her roadside stand on North Main heading out of town. Any kind of salty nuts, like roasted pecans, won't last long at my house. My wife likes a certain kind of cookie. Those didn't use to last long in the cabinet either, before she started getting back her girlish figure. How come it's so hard for us Americans to lose any weight? Most of us don't pig out; we just nibble.

I thought about having us do this food log where we keep track of what goes into our mouths. On the other hand, I'm not sure I want to know. I've given up sports and substituted water for coke. How's a guy supposed to have any fun around here? Munch, munch, munch.

I watched Raymond on <u>Everybody Loves Raymond</u> try his hand at managing the family checkbook. In short order he had it in such a mess that he ended up creating fake checkbooks and borrowing money from his brother to hide his screw-ups from his wife Debra. Just a few booboos here and there caused them to end up getting their power turned off. Flip, flip, flip.

I knew a guy I never believed could mess up. One day I heard they were splitting up. I was puzzled about it until I learned about a lapse in judgment by a normally wise man. You can eat an elephant one bite at a time, so I guess the Devil can do the same thing to a good marriage if it is not protected. I'm reminded that he goes about as a roaring lion seeking whomever and whatever he may devour. Slip, slip, slip.

A country can be guilty of doing the same thing. It's the old hand on the knee thing again. We fought for our independence and won. We fought a civil war that left scars forever, but our country finally held it together. More wars and conflicts tested us, but we're still here. Today we fight even more sinister forces that nibble at our national values and threaten to keep us from remaining a world leader capable of putting a man on the moon and exploring Mars. Chip, chip, chip.

It becomes a slippery slope as corrosive agents chip away at our base which eventually leak as with all dams holding back great pressure unless they are constantly monitored and repaired As also happens with friends and family members when we've seen changes for the worse right before our eyes, a country can repeat the past failures of great civilizations.

We learned in school how Rome and Greece both eroded from within before falling into ignomy. For many years now we have had the title of being the world's most powerful nation. How much longer can we say that. Snooze, snooze, snooze.

Many years ago a Frenchman named Alexis de Tocqueville visited early America. He said, "Not until I went into the churches of America and heard her pulpits, aflame with righteousness, did I understand the secret of her genius and and power. America is great because she is good, and if America ever ceases to be good, America will cease to be great."

I wonder if he returned to America today and made another run through our churches would he hear the things that once made us great, or would he see a nation in decline as he predicted would occur. Would those words echo off our half-empty church walls reminiscent of the empty cathedrals that I found in Europe as I went from town to town and country to country.

In the 1500's Martin Luther's hard fought battles against the Catholic church to bring life back to dying empty churches beginning the Protestant Reformation seems almost to have been forgotten by present day Western Civilization, including America. So soon we forget. Martin who? Too little too late I fear.

Fighting Back

Every year we try to watch <u>The Christmas Story</u> with Ralphie and the bully. We all cheer when Ralphie dispatches the bully, while Ralphie wears his bloody nose like a badge of honor. Too bad most bullying isn't that easily resolved.

My oldest son was a First Team All District high school pitcher and a three year letterman in college. He became discouraged his sophomore and first year as a starter in high school after a couple of the older players he looked up to started teasing him about something.

He drove a new sports car, had a job in our family business, and was nice looking, but the teasing/bullying hurt him. In time his mother convinced me to work with my son on the issue. Later he learned to deal with the pressure that comes with being the closer in college.

From these experiences my son today is a successful consultant in California and helps clients resolve issues to help them move forward in their lives. A friend of mine's child seemed to have a great life. Another child wrote bad things about the child on social media.

Just as puppy love is real to the puppy, a mole hill becomes a mountain to a young person in their myopic view of life. To them it literally can be and sadly sometimes is the end of their world.

It doesn't necessarily stop in the teen years. Remember Henry Winkler in the Adam Sandler movie where he battles his old college coach rival, Jerry Reed. In the movie he is able to come to visualize the bully as a baby and finally overcome his fear and domination by his old rival.

Have you heard that as many as 75% of Americans have some degree of glossophobia, a fear of public speaking. I knew a lady who dropped out of college her senior year as a 20 year old as she faced a speech class she had put off for three years. My wife eventually faced the paper tiger in her early 30's and became a successful and beloved elementary teacher.

She learned that any number of teachers love teaching their students but may break out in hives at parent orientation. Fear is a bully. It has no substance. It is hollow. When confronted it often dissolves, leaving us confused as to why we were ever scared of it at all. If you've had a college speech class you know that everyone is rooting for you and wants you to succeed. When you freeze up, you make the rest of the class more anxious than ever as they now envision themselves messing up.

Bullies can be your family members, bosses, classmates, or anyone else who can confront you and make you head to the bathroom with nausea or the big "D". The Devil wants to take the joy out of the lives of Christians. As a bully he uses many forms of fear to make us miserable. Maybe it's time we confronted one of those phobia bullies and make like Ralphie, even if it costs us a bloody nose.

Country Boy

Hank Williams Jr. or Bosephus sang a song, " A Country Boy Can Survive." It brought back memories of unforgettable early years on East Texas farms. The water came from a concrete cistern and later a rain tank. The light was provided by two kerosene lamps with sooty globes. A little upside down tank of kerosene behind the stove dribbled fuel for cooking. A wood stove heated the two room shack. The ice man made deliveries twice a week for the wooden ice box. Wet toe sacks kept the milk cans cool until Carnation picked them up early each morning. Several years later REA added electricity, but plumbing was still a ways off.

As Joe Friday used to say, "Just the facts, mam, just the facts." Those are the facts but not the memories. Hours on end were spent on my discarded broom with binder twine reins. Old Paint and I roamed the farm, cap gun in hand, loaded with caps for sound effects if I had any. We often ended up in our gulley where I faced the Dalton Gang and fended off Indian attacks. Our drink of choice was branch water without bourbon. I ate wild berries and persimmons. Muscadines with their thick skins replaced grapes, and "hicker" nuts picked out with bobby pins made delicious cookies. Sour dock and sheep showers were good to chew, albeit a little tart.

There was something peaceful about those days. I remember lying underneath the ironing board while Mama ironed and called out my spelling words. If I listen hard I might hear Murray Cox giving the Farm Report on KRLD. If he didn't say it, it wasn't so. In the evenings we were visited by The Lone

Ranger, <u>Cisco Kid</u>, <u>Sgt. Preston of the Yukon</u>, <u>Jack Benny</u>, <u>Fibber McGee and Molly</u>, and the <u>Great Guildersleeve</u>.

The smell of parched peanuts or sweet potatoes baking right out of the field—smothered in butter sloshed back and forth in a jug until your arms almost fell off—who needed dessert. I wished we had a churn back then. Homemade cornbread in a canning jar of cold milk recently from the cows—standard fare for Sunday night supper after stuffing ourselves at Sunday lunch on one of our fat chickens, especially if we had company coming. In that case I probably ended up with the neck. Speaking of necks, I gained a whole new appreciation for Mama's frequent phrase, "I'm gonna wring your neck." I gained a new admiration for the poor chicken who gave its all for Sunday company.

At school I saw my classmates playing with authentic motor graders and John Deere tractors under the cedar tree outside the cafeteria after lunch. Yes, I was envious, but in reality I enjoyed my blocks of scrap lumber and foot long bridge nails my dad got from building bridges. Sometimes farmers had to take extra work during lean times. I spent hours building multilevel structures and supervising knock-down drag-outs between my bridge nail wrestlers all the way from the Sportatorium in Ft. Worth as Bill Mercer whipped up the crowd. That might explain all those enjoyable summers in high school and college doing construction. Thankfully the wrestling fixation went away.

The good thing about being a kid is that everything is relative. My best friend and neighbor down the road didn't have a lot more than I did. We tramped over each other's fields and woods with bb guns and single shot .22. Skinny dipping in our muddy creek with snakes, crawdads, and snapping turtles was an adventure, especially if you survived with all your body parts intact. The stuff we did due to lack of good sense. Oh, but the fun we had. John Denver used to sing, "Well I wouldn't trade my life for diamonds or jewels; I never was one of them money hungry fools. Thank God I'm a country boy." Amen to that, John.

Hurleyville

That's what the sign says as you cross 515 heading south to Quitman. My mother told us kids once that Quitman got its name after one guy was pulling on another's big toe. He shrieked in pain, "Quit man." I can't verify that as the truth although it seems plausible. I do know Mineola was derived from a man's daughters named Minnie and Ola. Apparently they didn't like the original town name.

I don't know when Hurley's Store became Hurleyville. All my born days it was simply Hurley's Store, the hub of activity for that spot in the road. Before 515 was built running east to west, Hurley's was the closest store to the metropolis of Yantis. After 515 ruined our two meadows and made us drive our cows across the highway each day to be milked, I think Barney Curtis put in a store at the nearby intersection of 515 and 154.

Just the prospect of getting to stop there almost made me giddy. Dick and Melba Hurley were like members of the family. Dick was patient with me after Melba was hurt in a car wreck and confined to her bed for a while. As a six year old I flooded her with fresh tomatoes almost daily. She was only saved by my father's question, "Ya reckon she's got enough tomaters for a while, son." I don't know, I think I was in love with the prettiest woman I knew and only had buckets of tomatoes to express my infatuation. The fact that she was married didn't hit my 6-year old brain.

He was merely a bystander. My love could conquer all. Not sure how it all worked out. We probably shipped out the last of the tomatoes to some tomato shed in East Texas. Some loves have died a lesser death.

Hurley's store was the site of numerous drink-offs between my father and me. I think he pretended we weren't, but we really were racing. He got an "ROC" cola, and I got a Grapette. Forget the moon pie. As soon as he took a slug, the race was on. The only exception was when some Tom's peanuts were added to the deal. Pour 'em down the neck of that bottle and watch the salt cause the soda to bubble up and over. I don't think life got any better after a day in the field digging, pulling, or chopping.

Hurley's later added a feed shed to cover the shorts we bought to make bran slop for our pigs. We grew pretty much most of our cattle and horse feed. Sometimes we supplemented it with some Bossy or Purina feed. The sacks sometimes were colorful and ended up being sewn into clothes for us kids along with those made from slick flour sacks.

Most of us older folks grew up somewhere near a Hurley's Store. They were the source of knowledge of who's doing what where, who was sick, who needed a temporary hand, and about anything else. Old stores help hold the community together. Over the years my wife and I have tried to stop at every one we heard about. Often there were good lunches and breakfasts and "baloney" to be sliced, figuratively and actually. Sometimes the stores come in and then go out, all the while the community suffers. Anyone trying to make one a profitable proposition can tell you how hard it is to survive. Usually when the old folks stop running it, they often close. Not many young people are willing to tackle it.

If you have a mom and pop store/café in your little town, count yourself lucky. A haven for coffee drinkers and dominoes, it smacks of an era gone by. I feel about losing one of my favorite stores as I did about a special benefit I once had. I was dating a stewardess from the Metroplex whose dad had a big job with the perk of box seats at Texas Ranger games, which he generously shared with me.

As she was out of the country flying a lot of the time, I became very popular with my buddies at church as I frequently treated several of them to some great seats. After finally coming to my senses and going back to my future wife, a friend asked me if I missed my momentary love interest. I said, in typical manly self-interest, "Not really, but I surely do miss those box seats." Yes, us guys are all alike.

The Long Fight with a Short Stick

I was watching <u>Gunsmoke</u> the other day with a story about an old Sioux Indian who was left in a cave to die with dignity in his ceremonial robe. He spends the entire show trying to get back to the cave to die after being "rescued" by Festus who is unfamiliar with the Sioux tradition. The old Indian finally gets his wish as Festus comes to understand the Indian's desire to die with dignity.

My mother once told me she didn't want to die of dementia. After twenty years of suffering with it, she didn't get her wish. I reckon not many get to choose.

I've often wondered about dementia. It doesn't seem like we used to hear about it as much as we do now. As I visit the nursing homes each month to check on church members, I see the ravages of time affecting the dignity and quality of life as they're losing their battle for control of their minds. Going down the halls I see the names of rich, poor, famous, unknown, black, white, and brown on the name plates. Dementia is an equal opportunity destructive disease.

Through the miracles of modern science our medicines, therapies, surgical procedures, and preventative methods have greatly lengthened our life expectancies.

Our bodies are doing better, so much so that our minds seem to be wearing out first. As we watch our loved one go from forgetting keys to forgetting to breathe, it seems to be one of the cruelest of maladies. Early on the victim is aware of the changes in their mental processes but is helpless to stop it. No surgery, medicine, or therapies can alter the ultimate progress of the disease. We can pray for a cure or maybe the Rapture to spare us of this insidious predator, but that may not be in the cards for the near future. Until then we have to live our lives hoping those moments of forgetfulness are simply that and not the first stage of our mental demise.

There are medicines that may help slow the degeneration of our minds; improved eating habits may help our resistance; mental and physical gymnastics may help mitigate the attack somewhat. The truth is as with many other diseases, we just don't have the answers.

The last few years there were few visits to mom in the nursing home, including church staff and members. They feel it's not necessary anymore since the patient can't seem to communicate. I think that motivated me to visit the shut-ins and nursing home residents each month to at least let their family members know that they weren't forgotten. It's probably a small thing, but when it's a family member of yours, sometimes it's nice to know you're not alone when the person you love is going through that long dark tunnel in their mind.

Real Beauty

Who made up that scale? You know the one that ranks people based on beauty and physical prowess. It's probably always been there. We've always understood the shallowness of humans as they pick beauty queens based on outward beauty and outgoing confident personalities. Most Handsome and Most Beautiful tend to come from the same pool of candidates at school.

Sometimes we describe a person as being beautiful inside and out. Most humans are vain enough that it is hard for them to remain humble and kind when people are constantly fawning over them from an early age. Natural athletes can assume an almost godlike status growing up in a sports program at school. A drawback to all this adulation and admiration of these highly desirable physical features and accomplishments is an almost ironic result.

Rich people, popular people, athletic heroes, beauty queens, TV personalities, musicians, politicians, actors, and powerful people, be they locals or Fortune 500 CEO's, often have a problem bordering on paranoia. They love the status and attention that their popularity brings; however, then comes the issue of genuineness. What if I weren't popular or pretty? What if you lost your athletic ability? A friend of mine in high school was handsome, athletic, and popular. He was hit in the back and suffered kidney damage. He began to gain weight all over his body from the fluids. He did not look like his old self.

Fortunately he was well grounded and had a strong faith. Eventually his health returned. Having seen how his physical changes affected some former friends around him, he had a new appreciation for what mattered in life as he entered the ministry later. Two male friends of mine were handsome and virile and married to pretty wives. In separate wrecks one became disfigured, and the other lost the ability to have children. In each case the wives soon filed for divorce. Several factors could have contributed to these sad events. Maybe it was mere coincidence. Maybe the words "or worse" were left out of their vows.

Over the years I dated a couple of girls with Downs Syndrome siblings. In each case they were some of the kindest women I've known. Coach Gene Stallings from Texas A&M and the Dallas Cowboys included his son with Downs in all facets of work in football. I heard of a college coach recently whose son also was a Downs baby who grew to become a vital part of his college team as a manager and number one cheerleader for the team.

Many of you may have seen the great portrayal of a mentally handicapped team manager in the movie Radio. As in almost every instance I've seen or heard about people such as these, they seem to bring out the best in people around them. They are innocently honest and accept people for whom they are.

Again, almost in a case of strange irony, some people facing physical and mental challenges may bring out sincere and genuine love that we never knew we could feel. Maybe it was initiated by their honest and spontaneous love for us. That's eerily similar to a great Bible truth when we are told that Jesus first loved us, even in the womb he knew us. Yes, many of the beautiful and powerful people of the world can only wish that they could feel and know that people loved them for their real selves and not just the person that people think they are.

We've all heard about stories and seen Hallmark movies where famous people try to escape their fame momentarily in a small town, often at Christmas. The world looks at our outsides, while God looks at the heart. I've often wondered why He created people with physical and mental challenges. I've wondered why my mother had to suffer with dementia for 20 years. It finally came to me one day that it was for our benefit and growth as a person. The more we have the opportunity to serve others and come to see their real beauty, the kinder, gentler, more caring we can become. We all will eventually lose our physical beauty and skills.

When we recognize the real value of people's hearts, we finally are on the road to genuine love and inner peace. People who serve others, who the world doesn't always see as beautiful and worthy, are the ones who God has chosen to be blessed; they get the opportunity to reap eternal rewards by simply realizing what truly matters in a person. Sadly, those stuck on that treadmill of seeking approval and acceptance from a fickle world looking for the next shiny new thing may be the biggest losers.

For us ordinary mortals of average looks and abilities, we don't have to be told constantly how beautiful or talented we are. People care for us as we are. That's also how people who the world sees as physically and mentally different want to be treated. Regrettably, a world of people will never be able to move beyond the superficial world of appearances and finally discover the miracle of how God sent angels to us in human form, maybe different than we expected, to help us become the persons we were meant to be.

God said, "My ways are not your ways." Take heart regular folks. "For now we see through a glass darkly; but then face to face: now I know in part; but then shall I know even as also I am known." Hang in there. It will be worth it all.

Somebody's Listening

A while back at Christmas my oldest son gave me a notebook and pen with a note attached. It read, "The pen is mightier than the sword. Write away right away." As I entered retirement my son had written <u>DNA of a Good Dad</u> and using my words through his Captive Thought System secretly put together my first book <u>Serving Happiness</u>. The next year we worked together on my second book <u>Class Rules</u>. Over the first couple of years of my retirement he had me doing audio, video, and written blogs on Facebook on "Looking Up with Dr. Juan Harrison." As he got busier thankfully I was able to ease out of that. It was almost like work.

My youngest son before he ran for and became a new Judge wrote a great book called <u>The Great and Terrible Wilderness</u>, partly based on some of his adventures while serving as JAG legal adviser to a secret operation against terrorists in Southern Philippines. That campaign occupied my time for several months. After winning he then said we had to get me back to writing again. Why can't they leave me alone! Anyhow, he set me up on Facebook and now it's almost been a year of weekly, or should I say WEAKLY posts. Had I not first done the work with my oldest son and published the books, I doubt I would have agreed to doing my latest weekly post. Had my two sons not published books before me, I probably wouldn't have been a part of publishing mine.

My life has been rich and full. I still remember the boys in elementary school sitting in our playroom. One would be writing stories on top of a little desk and then sliding them down the toy box lid set up like a ramp. The second son proceeded to use his colors to illustrate the stories. It was a regular assembly line. My wife taught both boys early on to read and write. It was one of the greatest gifts she gave them, the gift of time as she quit her job to stay home with the kids. I started a side business, and we made it through.

I still remember when I went from education to working as Fuel Engineer for Texas Utilities for several years. Only working one job then let me set up a temporary office before computers in our laundry room. There I wrote on legal pads and typed on a portable typewriter my doctoral dissertation. There were times when the boys would come to my door with ball glove in hand and beg to play catch. More often than not I gave in.

I think what we taught them by example was how much we valued education and learning. We told them they had no limits. They saw us sacrifice as their mom went back to college in her thirties to get her teaching degree. They saw us set goals and reach them. Had we put the same amount of time and effort into her daycare or my landscaping business, it's possible we could have attained a fair amount of worldly riches. Instead, they saw the importance we placed on using our education to serve others. Consequently, one went into the ministry and the other into public law. We showed them and told them that service to others is what will make you truly happy. I think their mom and I are living proof of that. I always heard it's better to see a sermon than hear one any day. I'm glad their hearts were listening.

Willing and Able

It brought back up old memories, particularly the tough ones, from the early baby days. We were aware of the upcoming birth of the new grandbaby as we babysat Emmie while mommy went to her scheduled doctor visits. When the big moment arrived we took our designated spots, me at the hospital and Mamaw out to the farm to stay with number one while number two was arriving. In a short day or two everyone was back home trying to get used to a new routine we had almost forgotten about. We assumed the role of helper and food provider as we routinely would check to see what kind of food they wanted that evening or deliver any meals brought to us by their friends in town.

We became a supplier of diapers as Jack was going through almost one an hour. As the days passed we saw tired faces getting little if any sleep in the early days. Mamaw would come get Emmie for a few hours to give mommy a break, possibly napping when baby did. One concern we had was how Emmie would adjust to not being the center of attention. Fortunately she and the dog accepted the new pecking order.

Watching the kids deal with babyhood, this time with a toddler in tow, brought back some of the less pleasant memories we had of our own experiences as parents of newborns. Their sheer exhaustion from lack of sleep was bad enough. In the kids' case they had issues with septic system and the central heat/air during the most critical early days.

Throw in some sort of allergy/colds with the little ones, and you have an almost overwhelming situation. We ran errands for them, handled food, and took Emmie when needed. All the while they were adjusting to new parenthood, we kept reminding them that it would all pass. When you're in the eye of the hurricane you're just trying to survive each day.

I remember decades ago finding an exhausted young wife with a colicky baby at one a.m. Earlier both of our sons had been jaundiced early on requiring each one to stay in the hospital for a few extra days. That memory came back at Emmie's birth when she needed assistance with breathing after wearing herself out during delivery.

The effect of vicariously reliving our old memories from many years ago was churning stomachs and sleepy yawns. As with all things children, you want to take their worry; I stood next to my son 2 years earlier when I saw the concern in his eyes as six medical personnel rushed his infant daughter to the incubator to put her on a ventilator. When they hurt, we hurt. We would take all of this if we could. This is when we see the wisdom of God. He knows childbirth and childrearing is for the young. As we watch our children try to maintain normal lives and jobs, we can't imagine having to go through that again. These days we know that our strength and endurance continue to become more limited with age. Back then it seemed God gave us almost unlimited ability to get through it.

Fortunately for them and us our prediction that it will pass and they will survive finally does come true. Still, as they struggle and learn how strong they really can become when tested, we older folks say a silent prayer of thanks for God's grace in letting the young raise the young. We have a whole new appreciation for Abraham and Sarah in the Old Testament as they endured this as they approached a hundred years of age.

Remember Abraham's chuckle when told he was going to be a parent at his advanced age of 100. For me, that wouldn't have been a chuckle; that would be my last gasp for breath after my heart attack. I doubt I could see the humor in that situation.

Still, all things are possible with Him. I keep reminding the kids about that. As much as I anguish over the challenges and new responsibilities for them coming with parenting, I'm reminded of the joys and blessing that also accompanied it. Looking back I'd do it again. We've learned that God may not require us to go through Hell with a water gun, but He may want us to be willing to. OK, I'm willing. Just let me get my Geritol and oxygen tank.

Simple Man

I confess I am a simple man. I'm pretty sure there are a lot more out there like me. We love home cooking, but we understand when people are busy and eating out is a necessity or a mutually agreed on decision, especially when it lets Mama and me have a little extra time together to catch up on the day's goings on.

I don't ask for much. Give me a chance to work. Let me physically protect my family. Give me a decent wage to help meet my family's needs. Leave me enough in my check to help me care for family in time of illness. I don't need a mansion, just an opportunity to work toward having a place I feel safe in at night.

When I look in my pantry and see extra food I feel rich. Extra toilet paper, paper towels, laundry detergent, dishwashing pods —I remember a time when it wasn't so. I'm a simple man. Just a safe place to lay my head down in a place of love and peaceful rest will do me fine.

Give me the freedom to travel to old destinations I love, and new ones I may. Let my friends and family gather in love as we share Thanksgiving turkey and Christmas cider. May they sense the blessings on this modest domicile that can't be traded for mansions or gold. Memories have no price affordable to man. They make a house a home.

I don't need a new truck; I like my old one. I don't need many suits; one for funerals and to be married in and buried in and dress shoes are good. A couple of good shirts and some jeans will do. Most of the rest collect dust in the closet. A couple of fishing poles, john boat, maybe a deer rifle and shotgun for hunting game, a few tools in the shed to tinker with, don't have to be the best, maybe something to keep down the grass to appease the city neighbors or clean off the fence rows.

Make my chair soft and comfy. Don't fuss about snack crumbs in the floor. Make my tea sweet. Let our pets fill our laps or lie at our feet and comfort us with snoring when loneliness comes. Let my friends feel welcome for coffee and pie and a word or two.

I'm a simple man. I don't expect to change the world. I hope to leave it a better place. May my faith be more than words. May my actions put others before me.

May I always feel gratitude toward the source of it all and always be mindful it could go in a minute. As times roll on, help me to value more the important things and not waste time on the unimportant. Give me wisdom to know the difference. Life is simple. Keep the main thing the main thing. To all my simple brothers and sisters I pray you'll never give up the simple life for anything less. What you've chosen to pursue is far more valuable than earthly riches.

Making the Grade

I missed the course that trains you on how to raise kids. You tried your best, but you couldn't help wondering if you were doing it right. Teenagers and young adults rarely take the time to compliment you, but they tend to be pretty vocal or pouty if they think you've been unfair.

There was a phrase I finally got to hear when the youngest was almost out of high school when he and I were out of state getting Clay's sports injured knee examined by military doctors to get him cleared for his Air Force ROTC scholarship at the University of Texas. As we were driving back I casually asked him that on looking back if he thought I could have done a better job as a father. As was his usual tight lipped but direct approach, he simply said, "Dad, you did it right." I hoped he wasn't looking over my direction about then. Yeah, I've had a problem with allergies, son.

It's kinda scary to have to wait a lifetime for a report card. I was helping clean out a closet the other day when I ran across a box of newspaper clippings and memorabilia from Ryan's high school and college baseball days. My mind went back to the million miles and hundreds of stadium snack bar meals of hot dogs and nachos or Frito chili pies we consumed from here to Kalamazoo.

After he graduated from Dallas Baptist University, our car kept trying to turn in off of I 20 and run up the hill to the ballpark. Other sports parents I've talked to had the same sports withdrawal issues with their kids. I reckon just about any parent sending a kid to Tech, Baylor, or Austin or wherever has that feeling when you pass by the exit to the school. Tony Bennett may have left his heart in San Francisco, but you left part of your life and a small fortune in some college town somewhere.

On my 60th birthday I had to sit and watch a video with my staff and be embarrassed to see the kids and others say nice stuff about me. Clay repeated his "you did it right" mantra, this time from some far away country in his uniform. We worked really hard like most of you to give them every opportunity for a good start on life. It wasn't an insecurity that we had to give them a lot of stuff; it was the sense that we had to do everything possible mentally, spiritually, emotionally, physically, and fiscally to prepare them for the future by training them here today.

At times it did feel a lot like an acrobat walking on a rope or high wire in a Barnum and Bailey Circus.

Old age is not for sissies. Neither is middle age or any age when raising kids. In the classic movie Parenthood, a teenager played by Keanu Reeves, abandoned by his father, has a pretty succinct summary of our preparation for parenting; "You know, Mrs. Buchman, you need a license to buy a dog, to drive a car- hell, you even need a license to catch a fish. But they'll let any (expletive) be a father."

Good parenting is a skill acquired by experience and time. It helps if you have good role models, but every child is unique and requires an individualized approach. No one size fits all. We often refer to an "easy"child or a "difficult" child or "strong willed" child. The problem with child raising is we don't get an accurate appraisal on how we're doing until it's too late. I've often told friends that by the time the kids are juniors and seniors in high school, your house becomes a place to change clothes and maybe eat a bite. My youngest routinely got his meal at the local chicken place in case he didn't want what we had.

You pick your battles. At least he was eating. As you are helping them prepare to leave the nest, their involvement with sports, church, service clubs, and social life almost dominate their lives. If you haven't imparted life values to them by late teen years, it's virtually too late. You pray you did a good job, and if you're lucky to get a teenage to tell you as mine once said to me, "Dad, you did it right," you really feel blessed. Remember, I would never have known what he was thinking until I asked. Then, again, we better be ready to handle the report card if we ask.

Why Me? Why Not Me?

Once upon a time I said to an older friend that something wasn't fair. His comment was, "You want fair, go to Dallas." I did and I really enjoyed my Fletchers corn dog. My friend might be a tad cynical, but he probably learned a lot of things like you and I have the hard way.

Kelly Clarkson sang what doesn't kill you makes you stronger. Most of us have already or are going to have to endure some pretty tough experiences. People who have battled cancer or lost a child often tell me they don't know how anyone without faith in a higher power can get through it. None of the biblical heroes gladly went into a fish's belly or a lion's den. They were humans like us who got scared and ran away like Jonah or have amnesia like Peter when quizzed about his friendship with Jesus.

In my own life I have had events stretch my faith beyond what I thought possible. Our first baby was going to be Jamie Lee. I have a firm belief I will see Jamie in Heaven. I have been pulled and prodded into doing things I would rather forego. I've learned that God pays well. I've never done a spontaneous good deed that didn't end up with me getting some unexpected blessing. God won't be beholden to anyone. I have also learned that He is true to his word about being a much better and more generous Father to us than we are to our own children.

We're told that we see through a glass darkly. It's hard or impossible to get a good grasp of the big picture. We're told His ways are not our ways. Human wisdom is pretty weak, because we're told there's a way that seems right to man but the end thereof is death. That tells you how our human reasoning can even be fatal. He blesses our lives even when it doesn't look like a blessing at the time.

My niece died at 40 of cancer. At the end she told my wife she would go through it all again just to know how much her dad loved her as he carried her to and from her bed. My youngest tore his knee up in sports. He used the recuperation time to start a home Bible study group that reached 100 teens in our house and prompted a visit from my policeman friend asking them to hold down the praise and worship. One of the neighbors couldn't handle all that Christian fun. Lemons into lemonade we call it.

Attitude is everything. We choose to be happy. Having watched others and myself go through hard times has convinced me that God has to allow ordinary people to suffer, often seemingly unfairly, to demonstrate how a believer is able to survive the loss of jobs and family members. We become walking, breathing sermons showing others how they too can survive life's challenges. With the national suicide rate up 25% people are searching for ways to get through each day. The Bible tells us the rain falls on the just and the unjust. Bumper stickers remind us life happens.

Do we want to go through life never enduring bad things and missing the opportunity to grow as a person. If so, we're asking to be treated differently than the rest of the world. The issue is not if, but when. No it's not fair to have to endure hardship through no fault of your own. On the other hand, would you let yourself be used as Jonah, Mary, and Peter did. Look what examples and blessings we would not know about if each one above had refused to be used, fair or not.

Yes it's hard, but at least it's good to know someone will be there to help us through the darkest hours and bring us out into the light once more, this time willing to serve as a living sermon rather than empty sounds falling on deaf ears.

No Tears in Heaven

Revelation says, "And God shall wipe away all tears from their eyes; and there shall be no more death, neither sorrow, nor crying, neither shall there be any more pain; for the former things are passed away." Skeeter Davis sang, "No tears in Heaven , no sorrows given, all will be glory in that land; there'll be no sadness, all will be gladness when we shall join that happy band."

When you've been through the loss of a spouse, child, or someone close to you, the experience can be heart rending. A friend stood at the grave of his recently deceased wife grappling with the idea of never seeing her alive on this side of Heaven. That feeling of finality could be like an emotional straight jacket. The lifesaver is the knowledge that as believers we can be reunited in Heaven where tears don't exist. The things in life that bother us most --- tears, death, sorrow, or pain will not be present with believers in Heaven.

We partner with spouses for fifty, sixty, or seventy years on the earth. Then we go to Heaven where we are no longer partners.

The Bible tells us there will be no giving or taking in marriage in Heaven. We weep for our loved ones who go before us. In truth we weep for our loneliness and aching heart as they leave us for a place we can only dream of. It almost seems selfish of us, and maybe it is, but you literally feel you could die of a broken heart. I've watched my old friends lose a spouse only to die within months. Maybe it's a loss of will to live.

I've heard of partners of fifty or more years passing away on the same night even when not placed in the same facility. Loss can have a powerful effect on us; promotion to a place we can only dream of can be an even greater positive factor. Apostle Paul said after a life of suffering, beating, and deprivation," For me to live is Christ; for me to die is gain."

Paul is telling us that we have work to do on this earth as we suffer pain, sorrow, and tears. A relatively young friend of mine fought a long hard fight against cancer. She suffered other humiliation and emotional pain earlier in her life that may have seemed worse. She finally moved into the hospice phase. In no way do I think her friends and loved ones would want her to suffer any more. Humanly we'll miss her smile and great spirit.

She was beginning to get a glimpse of her new home. Shortly before she left from her earthly bed she began to move her arms in agitation. They tell me she was reaching out for the one who would go with her to that Promised Land where she can kiss her Kleenex and handkerchiefs goodbye. Johnny Cash sang, "When I come to the river at the ending of day, when the last winds of sorrow have blown, there'll be somebody waiting to show me the way, I won't have to cross Jordan alone. Jesus died all my sins to atone.

In the darkness I see, He'll be waiting for me, and I won't have to cross Jordan alone. Often times I'm weary and troubled and sad when it seems my friends have all flown. There is one thought that cheers me and makes my heart glad, I won't have to cross Jordan alone. Though the billows of trouble and sorrow may sweep, Christ the Savior will care for his own till the journey my soul will He keep, and I won't have to cross Jordan alone."

Stronger Together

At this writing in Thailand countries have sent help to try and rescue a group of boys trapped in a cave. In 2010 the world responded to rescue 33 miners from a mine in Chile. Whether it is a tsunami or earthquake, we see barriers dropped as the best in mankind demonstrates what can be accomplished when we work together.

There is no secret that a climate of conflict exists throughout the world. Countries struggle to control borders as refugees flee famine, danger, and have a desire for increased opportunity. Have nots seek to become haves. Aging countries and states struggle to find laborers to pick fruit, milk cows, drive trucks, provide healthcare, and teach our children. Our prosperity has created its own unique set of needs and concerns. We need roofers and construction workers and landscapers, but we struggle to meet the demand. Several friends of mine own trucking companies and can't find drivers as many of their trucks sit idle. Some have tried to train untrained drivers. They say they can't compete with wages in the oil patches paid to drivers.

We're talking about a good problem of prosperity in our country. When a country becomes prosperous people are able to focus on things other than just meeting basic needs. Maslow's hierarchy of needs goes from basic needs to self-actualization. As more people climb the ladder to success, people focus on quality of life, equality of opportunity for all, and finding personal satisfaction in our lives.

Past research has found that satisfaction rises until salaries reach a certain level. At the time the magic amount in America was about $70,000. After that, job and life satisfaction did not grow proportionally to further increases in incomes.

What we know is that serving others makes you happier. I gave a number of examples of this in my 2014 book <u>Serving Happiness</u>. The more we serve ourselves the emptier and more frustrated we become as material gains don't make us happy. Follow the lives of John Bulushi, Michael Jackson, Prince, Kurt Cobain, Marilyn Monroe, and the list goes on.

If people will look around for opportunities to make life better for others, our country and our world would become better places to live as people work together to address famine, poverty, and peace in warring countries. Hope springs eternal in the human breast.

Losing Control

Twenty minutes out of the Bonham VA I'm heading toward Commerce. The VA doctor made a couple of medicine adjustments and said he'd see me in 6 months. I'd had x-rays and lab done the week earlier, so I had time to work in a good breakfast at their cafeteria. Just out of Bailey on 11 the cell phone broke into my planning for the rest of my life. Dallas VA called to set up a CAT scan. I said there had to be a mistake. I had just seen my doctor who didn't mention it. I made them call my doctor who they said ordered the CAT scan. He in turn called me back. Yes, he said he didn't mention it since he thought Dallas was taking care of it. Yes, there was something dark, maybe a mass on the upper lobe of the right lung. No, I don't want a VA scan. I'll get my own at home. Yes, I know it would be free at the VA, but I'd rather use my local guys.

I drove straight to my civilian doctor at the clinic at home to get the ball rolling. I needed a doctor's referral. No, he's out of town at another clinic. I immediately drove to that one out of town and got the form to get the scan set up. The next morning bright and early I was at the radiology clinic's door, form in hand, hoping to " get er done." Not so. Doctor's notes sent in were incomplete. I walked back over to my clinic to goose 'em up. Won't be in until p.m. Left note to his nurse to get him to finish them so that it could be sent to insurance folks for approval.

The weekend was quiet. A couple of times I almost slipped and said something to my wife. I wasn't ready. I didn't know what to tell her. Fortunately she was babysitting Emmie one day and subbing at school the next. I kept thinking my face would show. Come Monday I figured I'd be safe for a couple of days even though they put "stat" on the scan request. I prayed they wouldn't call the house phone while she was there.

Yes, I thought about my wife and knew she'd be scared. I wondered how the boys would take it. Was it a dream or a nightmare? Was it only a false shadow or a mass? How did I feel so good with no pain, no breathing issues? Was it benign or not? Could they remove it as they miraculously had years before and saved my voice and half of my thyroid? Would I avoid chemo and radiation as I had before? I didn't even have to take medicine before because half of the thyroid was left.

We're headed north on 19 toward Paris on Tuesday. The phone rings in the car and radiology can't get the x-ray from the VA. Please come in and get one from the imaging center. I feel better already. I feel good knowing local guys will do a second one to confirm or contradict the first one. Yes, I can come early. Then we can expedite it to get insurance approval of the CAT scan.

My wife isn't mad as I secretly tried to get as much information and planning done before I had to overwhelm her. The phone call did it for me and her. At least I had had days to think about surgery, chemo, radiation, success, failure, and God's will in all this. My wife said I must be at peace to be able to fool her for the past few days. I did not want her to freak out any sooner than necessary. I was hoping to limit the time between x-ray, scan, biopsy, and a clear cut diagnosis with a realistic prognosis. I planned on waiting on the final word before I started on thoughts of surgery and recovery, if I were fortunate to get to use that word.

I didn't want to leave my family, my grandbabies. Yet I could see them later in Heaven, but honestly I still hadn't had enough earthly hugs and jelly fingers here. I had accepted whatever comes because I'd been blessed. Maybe I was a little greedy. I'd like just a little more quality time with family. There probably wouldn't be any negotiating. I hated to leave my wife and best friend to fend for herself. That saddened me. Yet, God could take what was meant for evil and turn it into good. His will be done. If it came down to it, you could leave a note in my casket. "Just one more kiss and hug, please."

P.S. I got the second x-ray done one week and the CAT scan a couple of weeks later. My faith and confidence had gone up and down depending on how human I'd felt. We'd only told a nurse friend in another town. She had regularly called to encourage my wife. My wife had been suffering in silence, but I saw the fear in her eyes as she tried to be brave. I was trying to keep up as good a front as I had in the posts I'd written about trusting God. Most of us know it's easier said than done when the rubber meets the road.

The phone rang in the p.m. after the morning's body warming IV that was hunting out the bad cells in my lungs. It was my family doctor. "I don't know who told you that you have cancer, but you just have some nodules that are pretty common. Might want to get the remaining half of your thyroid checked. It looks like some cysts in there. OK. See you in 6 months for another scan."

I hadn't wanted to tell family and friends bad news if I didn't have to. Now no need to get a friend or family member lined up to take over my customers for a while and no need to pull out any of my hard earned loot stashed in a rat hole to cover extra medical expenses. Didn't need anyone to cover my Sunday school class. Didn't have to dread that long recovery. Most of all, thank you Lord for grace. I didn't deserve it, but I'll gladly take it along with a few more jelly finger hugs and mac & cheese kisses. Maybe we'll get down to McDonald's playground yet and share some chicken nuggets. Little things add up to big things in the scheme of life.

Your PTO/Power Takeoff

Most tractors wouldn't be that useful without a good PTO/Power Takeoff. An engineer from International Harvester got the idea from a French farmer around WWI. It's designed to use the existing power of a tractor, truck, airplane or any number of engines or machines to do work more efficiently. Without it many pieces of equipment would not be as useful, and many jobs would be much more difficult.

Humanly speaking people have a lot of reserve power that is being wasted. Some people need to get their PTO checked and possibly overhauled. There is an unlimited amount of work out there to be done, but a lot of human engines are not equipped with an effective PTO to get it done. Larry the Cable Guy made the phrase "Get er done" a household term. Over the years we've called it "get up and go" and "gumption" or "pi_ _ and vinegar." We've often heard someone say my "Get up and go has done got up and gone."

The reality is that it's hard sometimes to get a stationary object moving again once it has stopped. Like the phrase "A journey of a thousand miles begins with a simple step" says, the first step is the hardest. Sometimes the problem is simply getting something unstuck. Floor wax and coats of paint can almost cement an old hutch to the floor. Once we break it loose then we can scoot it where we want to move it. We all have put off projects like cleaning out storerooms and closets for years. Some of us have a two car garage with room for half a car. Some of us got married skinny but the years have grown us. When we consider trying to reverse the process, the handle on

208

the Lazy Boy doesn't seem as easy to operate as we try to get up.

Our minds are powerful. They can tell you a million excuses to not engage your PTO. You get a comfortable routine: check the mail, get the paper, eat supper and go to sleep in the recliner, on the couch, or finally in bed. Our bodies aren't that excited either about changing routines. Procrastination can become routine. They call them resolutions for a reason. We have to resolve to stop doing something or start doing something if we are ever going to get that pesky task accomplished.

Whether it's going back to school, getting back in church, or starting that business, you have to engage that PTO. Once it kicks in, watch out. No telling where this story is going to lead.

Unaffordable

It's a small town. With social media the world is now a small town. There are no secrets anymore. If you had any, the kids tell them at school. When in doubt, the teachers always asked the kids about what was going on.

I never figured it out. Is it just selfishness? Is it the thrill of sneaking around? What are people thinking or simply not thinking? It's often people we've known for years doing stupid stuff because they can. Nice people, "good "people. Some are predators with positions of authority. Some people are flattered to be asked but shouldn't be. These guys hit up ten others before you. Did you think it would get you that career advantage? Were you afraid not to? Did spouses pretend not to know?

I heard a woman made her husband pay for his infidelity with house renovations and newer cars. These predators are people living in houses we envy and in cars we value. How do their spouses do it? Our friends know about it. Probably the kids know. Still, people stand by their mates. Were they afraid to leave the big houses? What part of their soul were they willing to trade to keep up appearances and maintain their lifestyle? I understand the vow, "till death do us part," but the living death inflicted by the serial cheater eats away at the very core of the betrayed spouse. I was encouraged years ago when I saw one local lady tell her habitual philanderer to take the lifestyle and shove it. She chose personal integrity over selling out for stuff as she left town. I know it's not that simple, but I can't understand not caring more about how you feel about yourself. Peace of mind is worth something.

How can a person let a partner do the most personal act you can commit with someone else and then let them come home and expect to resume their old role. You actually risk your physical health. I'm a man. I can't understand this. Is there some eternal hope that the offender will change and never do it again? Who's kidding whom? The leopard rarely changes its spots. It's a lifestyle, a habit. Something is missing in the heart of the man or the woman, whoever is unfaithful. I believe in forgiveness, but at what point does a woman or man finally say, "Enough. I care more about myself than to let you use me as a home port while you sail out to unknown shores." It looks like people are trading stuff/position/lifestyle at the expense of self-respect, personal integrity, and laughter behind their backs.

Fear of material loss, risk of embarrassment, or desire to keep a certain lifestyle can tempt a person to compromise and sell their soul. Do you say you do it to protect the kids? The kids know more than you think. What are you teaching them about self-respect? Do you stay together to avoid embarrassment and loss of social status? Maybe you put up with it because you don't think you can survive without him or her? Perhaps you finally gave up and lost yourself? You ask yourself how did it get this far. You wonder is it time to get out. This isn't what you had in mind when you said, "I do." You asked if lying to self has become the norm. You've started thinking that the price of status quo has become too high. It feels unaffordable. Some things are worse than being alone. A healthy person must keep what self-respect is remaining. Maybe it's time to save what sanity is left.

Silly Man

I think I must be a simple man. No smart aleck comments or I'll refer you to 2 Tim. 3:6 (KJV) reference to "silly women." More modern versions say "gullible." Anyway, I was between mowing jobs parked under a tree in the Bowie School driveway eating my dollar McChicken sandwich, free medium water and listening to the Bee Gees in my El Camino. I'm thinking it doesn't get much better than this. Who cares that we were under a heat alert.

In 1st Timothy 6:6-12 Paul says, "But godliness with contentment is great gain. For we brought nothing into the world, and we can take nothing out of it. But if we have food and clothing, we will be content with that." In Philippians 4 he says, "Not that I speak from want, for I have learned to be content in whatever circumstances I am." That's pretty good coming from a guy who spent time in prison and was left for dead just for telling about how he went from prosperous Pharisee to living as a tentmaker to survive.

I'm thinking this is one of those lessons you and I don't wanna volunteer for. Think Jonah and what it must have smelled and felt like in the belly of that fish with other decaying matter all around. Almost anything after that would seem like a piece of cake. I know after I was buried up to my chin in cottonseed meal in a tank at Farmers Co-op in college and lived to tell as another wall of meal was threatening to bury me, I wasn't quite as gripey about my server in a restaurant.

Remember the parable of the successful farmer in Luke 12 who had a bumper crop. Rather than being content he decides to tear down his old barns and build bigger barns. The only problem is that God called him a fool. He said, "This very night your life will be demanded from you. Then who will get what you have prepared for yourself?" A person once asked me what made God laugh. I immediately thought about my hair in the morning after I had been rooting around on my pillow all night. Think Alfalfa from Our Gang or Alfred E. Newman from Mad Magazine. Wrong. The correct spiritual answer was "men making plans." I guess I wouldn't make a good Pharisee.

I met a man once who lived on the plains in Africa. I asked him what issues he had as he worked with the poverty stricken tribesmen. He quickly said, "Envy." I choked on the jelly bean I was eating. "What" was all I could squeak out. He said the guys in grass huts want stick huts. The guys in stick huts want mud huts. It sounds like a version of "Three Little Pigs" and the wolf. I thought we're not a lot different here. A lot of us get a starter home or mobile home with plans for a bigger or larger place. We may move 3 or 4 times before we finally settle for our house that we retire in. Low and behold some of my buddies say now it's time to downsize. The place is too much to take care of, all the while people are driving past drooling wanting a place like that. Bigger barns. Is "fool" too strong a term, or do I dare challenge the American Dream a lot of us spend our lives chasing. Silly men.

Clean Underwear

We talked here while back about how bullies are often paper tigers built up by fear in our minds. In a similar vein, things said and done to us often have a much greater effect on us than they should. As we've repeated many times in life, remember the bumper sticker, "Stuff happens," or some variation of it. Now what? How do you react to it—divorce, cancer, child stops talking to you, get rejected for a job or told you're too old, too fat, too skinny, too short. What do you do? Ninety-five percent of the stuff can't be helped. Not much you can do about the other five. How you react is up to you. I'm not using this as an excuse for my mess-ups, but my favorite phrase I use whenever I've been passed over, passed by, given up on, shot down and generally done dirty or wrong is simply, "Your loss."

I'm not talking simple arrogance here. I'm telling you that you need to throw it back on them with a simple thought, "Your loss." You know had you been picked, not rejected, you could have made all the difference in the world in the job, the marriage, the club, the choir, the team. They didn't pick you; they let you go—their loss. I love George Strait's song "She Let Herself Go." It tells us about a woman who finally got out of a bad relationship and then let herself go—not gaining weight from taking solace in chocolate and bonbons, but getting even by finally finding some joy in life with some spas and trips to the beach she had been deprived of. The result was what I called the greatest form of revenge—success. George says she came back "knocked out pretty." You get the feeling some guy is wishing he hadn't been so hasty in letting her go. I don't think crocodile tears are going to bring her back. She's gonna find someone who maybe like her got taken for granted.

How many times have you seen someone taken for granted or ignored in a relationship when others outside the marriage are dying to have someone of that quality for a partner and best friend. Too many times people have to cry in their beer and sing the line "You don't know what you've got till it's gone." Again, I'm not talking arrogance here. I'm simply saying too often people, even family members, sell us short. We've all heard, "If you don't believe in yourself, who will?"

We pretty much tell people how to treat us. In most cases people can't do to you what you won't allow. Maybe husband, boss or family members have convinced you you're not worth much. You can buy that or prove em wrong. You know down deep that you do matter and can make a difference. You know spiritually that a great price was given for you. You also know the old phrase, "God don't make no junk." A good hard, honest look may need to be taken. If you like how things are going, no problem. If you're ready to be treated with respect and appreciation, then take inventory. You might be surprised to find there's a world waiting out there for a confident you ready to contribute and make a difference. Once you rev up those engines and kick in the afterburner, they better move over. They say the world steps aside for the man who knows where he's going. I say the world better get ready for the woman who probably had to tell the man where he was going and remind him to wear clean underwear.

Living With Yourself

Modern technology has almost made living with yourself a dying art. When you see 4 friends or family members sitting in a restaurant not speaking but focused on their phones, you know our society is being transformed and not necessarily for the better. With access to instant entertainment constantly in your hands, no one has to endure silence. It is almost like having a phobia of time to think and consider things.

A number of experts have used the word addiction in relationship to our phones. People take them to bed with them and keep them and other devices constantly close to them on vacations. Part of it may be the desire to appear busy or remain busy. Some people who are constantly eating may do so to fill up their time and feel they are occupied rather than making healthier, more productive use of their time.

I've worked outside a lot over the years. I like the time to think and consider things. It gives me ideas for writing. No one bothers you when you're operating equipment, so the work gives me uninterrupted time to work out problems and reason out ideas. If I don't want to think, I can put on a headset. Otherwise, it's a peaceful time to mull things over to consider pros and cons as I make decisions.

I believe to be at peace with yourself you have to really get to know yourself and accept who you are, warts and all. Other people can entertain you, but only you can truly make yourself happy. We know that money, things, even good friends can only do so much. Aristotle once said, "Knowing yourself is the beginning of wisdom." Accepting ourselves and forgiving ourselves helps us to come to accept and like ourselves. Eating alone and even watching movies alone doesn't have to be miserable times but can give us time to observe and learn. We think people may look at us funny for doing things alone, but the truth is they don't care and are more interested in their own issues. We often give too much thought to what other think about us when in truth they generally don't. Most people are so occupied with their own thoughts that we are secondary thoughts.

A person can be lonely living with someone; ask any number of married people. One doesn't have to be lonely by herself. Ask any married housewife who craves a few moments of silence during her hectic day. Time alone can be recuperative and healing. Our happiness does not have to depend on constantly having other people around. It is a choice we make. A person can know himself, trust himself, and like himself. We need to get off that phone and engage that brain. There is a world out there to observe and enjoy. If we find someone to share it with, great. If we don't, great. We win either way.

A Better Gift

It is too simple but it works. Gratitude. Some people say we need an attitude of gratitude. Others say God is good all the time. What I do see is a decline in common civility where people say "please" and "thank you." Have you ever seen an almost shocked look on someone's face when you genuinely show your appreciation to someone, even a stranger? A lot of us are not used to hearing those words.

Ever thought how it feels when you do a good deed, and someone says, "God bless you," and you didn't even have to sneeze. You can't put a money value on it. It's like the kids or grandkids stopping by without being asked to, or maybe getting a sweet kiss from the little grandchild. We live for these moments. We hunger for people, especially our families, to appreciate us. We don't really expect it, but nothing makes you work harder than knowing someone cares and appreciates what we have done for them. Somehow hearing those words and knowing they are genuine makes all the overtime, second and third jobs, and getting called into work a little more bearable. In marriages we often hear someone say they're tired of being taken for granted. Wives work outside the home and still work inside the home and may never hear anything but, "What's for supper?" That sounds like Frank talking to Marie on Everybody Loves Raymond.

We know that expressing gratitude and appreciation to people can't hurt and may actually help make other people willing to go the extra mile for us. Again, it is a simple thing, but it can pay big dividends. Some of us more human types around powerful, affluent people sort of selfishly hope by being nice to them that they might at least tell someone how nice we are or maybe bless us some way.

Listen to what the Bible says about God wanting to bless us, "If you then, who are evil, know how to give good gifts to your children, how much more will your Father who is in heaven give good things to those who ask him! So whatever you wish that others would do to you, do also to them, for this is the Law and the Prophets."

When we are kind and appreciative to others, blessings will come to us. When we do good deeds unselfishly, we will be blessed by God. He will not be obligated to or outdone by you. Sheer gratefulness and kindness to others opens the flood gate of blessings. These will exceed what humans would do because they are coming from a heavenly Father. Whatever we do or say to help bless someone's life will be multiplied and returned to you in abundance; better than a Roth IRA or 401K and paying much better interest.

The Money Trap

Over the years I've heard of spenders and spendthrifts in a marriage. Not surprisingly one of the top reasons couples give for divorce is financial issues. We don't hear a lot about that or see many Lifetime movies about it. It's not glamorous or sexy; it is real life. Some marriages work by letting one person manage the finances. If both people are careful with money, then they can focus on other areas of the marriage. If both people are spenders, then Katy bar the door!

How often have you sat and listened to a friend lament their precarious financial condition, then you see on Facebook or hear from the person about something they bought or a trip they took. Most of us ordinary people find it a challenge to meet obligations, much less spend money we don't have. It almost seems like those guys who want it all now are having all the fun, yet, next thing we know they're telling us a sad new story. You may even have helped them out of a spot, but you know it's putting money into a dry hole.

Fighting debt and financial issues is an ongoing thing. I call it a spiritual ailment; it "sticketh closer than a brother." Once the honeymoon is over and the first rent is due, a young couple begins to see the reality of it all. If they don't have agreement on finances, little wedges start widening little cracks in your little ship of love. The hugs and kisses can only go so far.

I remember as a newlywed paying $125.00 a month for our first apartment and seeing big roaches having parties at night in our kitchen sink. We soon climbed up to a nice apartment for $160.00 a month, swimming pool, laundry room, and no roaches. Her $35.00 a week she made at the car lot while she drove to college in my new car she confiscated was pretty much our weekly grocery budget. I knew I married the right one when we were on the honeymoon to Eureka Springs/Branson as we approached our last day there. I told her we could stay the last day with no money for groceries, or leave today and buy some food. She chose the food. The stewardess I was dating before her might not have made that choice. Later circumstances confirmed I had made the right choice for me. Thank you Lord for giving me grace.

Christians believe the Devil is behind the pressure on people, old and young, to get what they want now. Clouds of debt riding on your head as a newlywed is not nearly as enjoyable as the sensible couple taking it slowly, cautiously. You can eat the elephant one bite at a time; just don't try to swallow the whole thing.

I think the financial issues in marriage are often just a symptom of a bigger problem. The key may be unrealistic expectations. Heck, you buy all this stuff, then both of you work yourself to death for things you're either too tired or too busy to enjoy. Surveys have told us that women working full-time outside the home and still doing most of the housework leaves some pretty tired women. The women often stated their greatest desire was to get more sleep, not, you know what. Sorry fellas, I just report the news. It is not realistic that our frantic pace of living won't take its toll. My mom used to say that young couples don't even have time to finish arguments. Even the kids are busy, busy. Maybe it might be a good time to see if we could unclutter our lives a little and reduce some financial obligations. Good luck hunting.

The Spice and the Rub

They say opposites attract. That seems common in marriage. People seem attracted to mates who are often stronger in areas where they are weaker. Most people realize how boring it might be if spouses were your clones. For good marital cooking you need the spice each one provides. What gives us spice can also cause sensitive feelings to rub and cause heartburn.

The divorce rate is over 50%. For people living together before marriage statistics are worse. Second marriages fail in the over 60% ratio and third marriages break up over 70% of the time. Putting two people together with opposite personalities is a challenging situation. Given enough time couples can begin to rub off edges. The problem is that time is also the foe. One third of marriages end in the first 5 years. Young couples lack the wisdom and experience needed to put differences in perspective. Compromise is becoming a lost art. If they focused on each other's strengths instead of weaknesses and served each other first, survival chances improve.

Marriages of 50-70 years are getting rarer. Couples were not able to have such longevity without having some secrets for their success. Words like compromise and give-and-take don't seem as popular in general in our society, including marriage. Conflict is on our roads and in our state houses. Today's marriages face a pressure cooker climate compounded by the demands for instant satisfaction.

Older marriages survived on sacrifice and patience. They cared more about the partner than themselves. Younger people coming into marriage often demand their way first. Patience is a rare commodity. Expectations are often high, if not unrealistic. They may set unreasonable deadlines with little room for flexibility. They frequently expect too much and selfishly demand too much of each other. They often don't practice forgiveness of each other. Most humans couldn't and sadly don't measure up to these demands.

A lot of people believe marriage is going the way of the dodo bird. They don't know or haven't experienced the benefits of a good marriage based on security and trust. Fewer people have been raised or seen solid families where everyone benefits from caring family members. They have fewer role models of happy marriages after which they can pattern their marriages. Many are flying blind.

To reverse the trend of broken marriages and their aftermath, young people must make an even greater commitment to do what is necessary to build and hold on to their marriages. If each partner in the marriage can practice forgiveness and have more patience and realistic expectations, these young people may be fortunate to experience the blessings of good marriages as they work hard to beat the odds of present marriage trends.

Unleashing Your Potential

You don't need to touch the TV. You don't need to send seed money to prove your faith. There are some easy steps to end your sleepwalking through life and missing out on some great experiences. Successful living occurs when preparation meets opportunity. Far too many of us are missing out on great blessings, and it's our fault. The tragedy of it all is that we don't know that we don't know.

All around us are miracles and blessings waiting to occur. The book of James says, "Ye have not because you ask not." The potential for personal and societal change is limited only by ourselves; 2 Chronicles tells us, "If my people, which are called by my name, shall humble themselves, and pray, and seek my face, and turn from their wicked ways, then will I hear from heaven, and will forgive their sin, and will heal their land."

Our land is in need of healing; it is suffering from multiple forms of sickness reflecting a deeper problem. Prescription addiction, overeating, personal bankruptcy —all resulting from a personal lack of responsibility and total focus on self. Our country's total obsession with "me first" has made us totally oblivious to the world around us. While contemplating our navel we are ignorant of the possibilities and needs of the world around us. We have created this mess and now have the opportunity to effect change that could result in blessings to the actor and the recipient.

Insanity is doing the same thing over and over and expecting different results. Lives of failure have resulted from blindness to the needs of others and also of ourselves. Contrary to human wisdom, the key to happiness can only come from serving those around us. Serving others brings blessings and helps meet the needs of those around us struggling to find meaning and purpose in life. Proverbs tells us, "Where there is no vision, the people perish." It is critical that we open our eyes and help others see a vision of life that has meaning. Headlines detail the plague of suicides as people without hope perish.

Serving self is death; serving others is life. Our country is on life support. Pockets of light across our land give us hope that it is possible for the American people to fulfill their destiny as a special blessing to the world and a protector of an ancient people of destiny. It must begin here and transpose itself to the rest of the world. What we know is that God wants to bless this country. He says He will bless us for our support of a blessed people. It's simple. Serve others here and around the world and create a tsunami of hope for this land. Serve ourselves and watch our country die from within as Greek and Roman empires did before us. This miracle country was created for special purposes. We must be a blessing to others. If not, we have no legitimate reason to exist.

What Women Want

Here while back I heard about a survey where women rated more sleep as higher priority over men's wishes and put "me" time or any kind of uncommitted time at the top of the list. I'll give the guys a few seconds to get over bruised egos. As awesome as us guys are, we probably already knew how the survey would turn out.

If we're fortunate to stay married long enough to peel the onion back more than a petal or two, us guys have probably begun the process of discovering how complicated women are. It doesn't get much easier after years of marriage. " Let's eat. Where? You pick. No, I picked last time." That's just for starters. You'd think I won the Nobel Prize when I guessed right and secretly decoded the right eating joint she preferred after all.

With forty years in the mirror and time on our hands, we're both still alive, have a modicum of brain cells left, and have the freedom for occasional road trips. We go, we talk, we look at things we missed before. I think she likes this time with me. I sense I'm a lucky man.

Then again, she loves her friends and trips with them. I'm happy for her and the time they have to spend with her. They meet needs I can't fulfill and don't attempt. We love the time apart. She's the trip planner and reservations expert for the girls. I'm liking staying home and doing my little business. A certain amount of absence can make the heart grow fonder. I help keep her in a decent ride and don't hassle her about what she spends. She knows how much is I there as well as I do. There are bigger fish to fry.

It seems that my wife needs the security of home and the knowledge that I trust her and vice versa. She needs the fellowship and support of her 8 best friends. She likes to go and loves the phone. I told her to cover up some pillows on my side of the bed and she'll never know I'm gone. Seriously, I want her as confident and prepared for my departure as she can be. I used to hear of bosses who would slip outside doors of their office so the employees wouldn't know they were gone. I went out the front door; I wanted the place to run as good without me. At the coal mine as a Fuel Engineer I would fill in for foremen as we loaded those 80 cars of coal for the power plant at Monticello. Bosses told me the guys would sneak around and hide behind the giant stockpile of coal. I trusted the guys to keep doing their jobs. They didn't let me down.

Women want what men want. They don't want to be the man; they want to feel like partners and be given credit for the contributions they make to a relationship. I learned long ago the best way to get and keep good employees was to give them credit when credit was due; let them get recognized for their efforts; let them feel free and confident to try new ideas without fear of reprisal if they failed. By accepting failure as a part of marriage or any relationship, we acknowledge that we're all human.

Last but not least, she wants to be free to laugh at herself when she fails and forgive others when they fail. By being free of the baggage and garbage of failure, we make room for more joy and happiness. All any of us want is to be accepted for who we are, warts and all, and if we're lucky, maybe even be loved along the way. It worked pretty good for a guy named Jesus. You can't hardly improve on perfection.

Things He Missed

Early in my life my father left us for another family. The immediate effect on us as it has been economically on many other single parent homes was a state of near poverty. Mom went to sewing blue jeans to feed and house us. We kids found work to help mom make ends meet. In the late 50's and early 60's I was embarrassed to tell folks my parents were divorced, which was a rarity among kids I knew and girls I dated. When my date's father would ask what my father did for a living, I'd tell them he was dead, which was kinda true because he was dead to me.

As the years passed and the pain eased, I began to get a healthier perspective. Mom did an admirable job of filling both roles and making us feel safe and secure. We worked so hard to keep things afloat that there wasn't much time to feel sorry for ourselves.

As mom cheered for me at all my home games, I began to ponder some things. Life had gone on for us. My dad had made his bed; soon he found his bed was hard and lonely. There was little time or interest for sympathy for him from our family. To my knowledge he never attended any of my ballgames. My mother's cheers were unmistakable. His were silent. How could a father miss out on such events like that. I vowed never to do that with my sons. His loss.

As time passed, so did opportunities for him to be involved in our lives. High school graduation was followed by college graduation from Tech. My favorite lady college professor filled in as she pinned on my Air Force officer bars. Other fathers were there to help honor their sons. There was little time for boo-hoos over spilt milk. It kept running through my mind—another addition to the list of things he had missed. It culminated with Mom seated alone at my wedding. By then any feelings for Dad were long gone with zero contact from him. My last memory of him until I stood at his open grave with only my four sisters and mother present was a phone call from the Lamar County Sheriff's Office telling me they had picked him up homeless on the side of the road in the rain. Did I want to come get him? No, I hadn't seen him in years. He was a stranger to me now.

As my children were born and had their ballgames and birthdays, I wondered if he ever thought about what he missed. His grandsons never got to hear him cheer for them or take them for ice cream after a game. He wasn't there at the Capitol to pin on Clay's officer bars or watch him toss his mortarboard into the air at graduation at UT. He also missed his grandson's graduation from Baylor Law School where he failed to see his other grandson pitch against the Baylor Bears. Parents and grandparents get to invest time and resources into their offspring. They get repaid with championship games, graduations, officer commissioning, and births of grandkids. No investment; no rewards. The other grandfather proudly has my oldest son Ryan's championship college ring on a shelf on his wall. In life we get opportunities to be a part of the lives of others. If we pass them up, someone else will step in to fill the gap and reap the relationship rewards. God tells us He will be a father of the fatherless and a protector of widows. In my lifetime He sent many men into my life, from my neighbor John Crowson who played catch with me to Audley Moore and Son's Construction who called me in on a cold winter day to tell me they would guarantee me work in high school and college any time I had a break. Mrs. Lela Raines took me fishing every chance she got; she had a gate key to half the ponds in Hopkins County. Now that's a valuable friend and fill-in grandmother.

Life is about investing in others. If we pass up those opportunities someone else will replace you and reap the benefits. I have no feelings about the father who missed all those opportunities to be in his son's life. It was my father's loss. I'm doubly grateful to the men and women who stepped forward to fill the gap. I hope my wife and I have been faithful in helping other young people when they needed a hand. I do know my own sons were the direct recipients of parental love motivated even more by watching a living example of what not to do; I also know the blessings and rewards that come when you choose to invest in the lives of others. We become fill-in fathers to some and stronger fathers to our own children than we might normally have been.

Little Bitty

Alan Jackson sang "It's alright to be little bitty, a little hometown or a big old city." A lot of us country folk understand what he means. Not all of us can go back home, make a living, and return to the roots of our raising. A good number of my peers have come back home in retirement having missed the working years here often living in a "big old city." At least they had the good sense to get back home. They probably had to get used once again to seeing complete strangers smile and greet them or wave or nod their head as a lot of us guys do. My friends from up north have questioned our habit of "driving friendly" as the license plate said. I even had a California lady question my sincerity as she heard me greet a stranger with our usual "How's it going?" I just smiled at her. It's not something you think about; you just do it.

Once on Andy Griffith the citizens of Mayberry, normally a friendly North Carolina hamlet, got upset when a former soldier got off the bus and started walking up to people, greeting them by name, only to be met by strange looks of suspicion. Andy was able to quell the furor by finding out that the soldier while serving overseas began to read a fellow soldier's Mayberry weekly newspaper with names and pictures in it. Turns out that the young man didn't grow up in a little bitty town where, like Cheers, everybody knows your name. He just wanted to settle down in a place where he felt a part of the community.

Little bitty life doesn't mean you have to be poor. It just means living a life where you matter and where others matter to you. Bobby McDonald, a local accountant/tax preparer was that kind of guy. His dad Pete lost a foot in the Korean War but still managed to teach me to swim in his pond. Bobby produced his own online newspaper called Front Porch News. A lot of times he scooped the local paper or enhanced their stories. Bobby helped make the community closer by giving us details on people and events in our little town.

In my hometown, people don't have a lot of use for snotty people. We're mostly just folks who like our Relay for Life, Hopkins County Stew Contest, Fall Festival and Dairy Festival Parades, our Indian days and Dutch oven cooking at Heritage Park, our 4th of July concert on the square and a million other local events. We may be little bitty, but we develop great support for cancer fighters and victims of house fires. We put colorful signs in our yards and flowerbeds indicating our partnership with their battles so they won't feel alone. We may not have a big old house or a sack full of money, but we have a feeling we'll be missed when we're gone because we all contribute in some way to the feeling of community in our little bitty town. John Donne once said "No man is an island entire of himself." If we listen to the 12:30 news and don't hear our name on the list of obituaries, it's a good day. That gives us another shot at helping a neighbor or friend or maybe a newcomer to our town in need of a friendly greeting or some banana nut bread. Ain't nothing wrong with being little bitty. All that stuff people are chasing is pretty much meaningless. What matters is the size of our hearts.

Relative Wealth

Over the years I've related to some of you about an encounter with a friend that really helped put my life into perspective. She was an "old maid" living in the family home. Her mom had passed. She drove an older vehicle and had no serious hobbies. Understandably, with few expenses she had a large balance in her bank account. One day she stopped by my office for a short visit. As we finished, she got quiet for a moment. She then asked me, "What do you want to do with your life?" Half-joking, I said, "I'd like to be as rich as you." Her face took on a serious look, and her eyes were tinged with sadness. She leaned over my desk and almost whispered, "You are rich." In a brief moment I understood. She had no husband, children, or grandchildren. Her life had a routine but was not being shared with another person in her home. I had a life brimming over with children and grandchildren and a good wife to share it with. As my friend said, "You are rich."

Have you ever stopped for a minute to think about your life and what you've been blessed with. I know a majority of us would be in deep do-do if a couple of months passed with no income. A recent poll said a majority of Americans couldn't come up with a thousand bucks in a pinch. A thousand dollars doesn't buy nearly what it used to.

What is real wealth? Is it the instant loss of something that made grown men on Wall St. jump out of tall buildings in 1929 at the beginning of the Great Depression? Is it something you can't put your finger on but is powerful enough to make us grown people get up early and work late to provide a safe place called home for people we care more about than ourselves?

Real wealth: a hug and kiss from a grandchild; a thank you from a grateful child; a lick on your hand from a good dog. It's like a reason to live. I love my wife; I live for the kids and grandkids. She feels the same way. After the first grandchild hit town, she explained to me where I fit in the relationship chain. Guess who had moved to the top. Grandparents get it. It's kind of like unconditional love without all the rules we had raising our own kids.

The saddest thing in this life is to become an older person and not have acquired the knowledge about what is truly valuable, what endures. It's not the Chevy truck, the Kubota tractor, or the beautiful lawn. What we invest in is what gives us lasting dividends. The value of gold, silver, and oil go up and down each day. Jesus said, "Do not lay up for yourself treasure on earth, where moth and rust destroy and where thieves break in and steal." Remember, for some people it isn't that we don't know; it's the fact that we don't know that we don't know. It's hard and scary to change when we are older. May God give us the wisdom to see what is important and live our lives accordingly.

More Than A Bed

"Mamaw, Papaw, here," as her 2 year old finger pointed down the hall to our bedroom. Assume your positions as Emmie crawled up the ottoman. "Papaw." I wasn't moving quickly enough. She's in the middle of the king size bed, ready to bounce. I've always just thought of it as a bed; now it's a trampoline with human rails to prevent disaster. We'll never be able to look at it the same after her gymnastics exhibition.

It got me thinking about how it wasn't simply a piece of furniture. In some ways it's almost a part of the family. At night after a long day, that cool, welcoming pillow and soothing sheets seem to say, "Welcome home." Good old dependable mattress with the hump in the middle between our 2 personalized hollowed out recesses awaits our "aahs" as our bodies lie down for a well-deserved rest. As time has gone on it's gotten harder to climb up that mountain to kiss good night. More often it's "Love you." I repeat, "Me, too" or maybe I start the refrain. She's less lazy with her " Love you, too."

Life has started there; it will end there if God is gracious. It was the fortress of safety and security as the little ones would crack open the door after a nightmare, sweetly telling us of their fears as they piled into the middle of us. We'd spend the rest of the night dodging flying feet and arms. More than once I'd retreat to the couch or another bed. Truth be known, sometimes we'd both end up in their beds and vice versa as we struggled to get enough sleep to get us through the work day. Parents of the young remember the crying, grunting, rooting little bodies that ended up with you as you tried to get through another night. Exhaustion often became a close companion. We were young and survived. Not sure how that would go today. Entertaining and cleaning up the trail of toys is a faint reminder of our higher energy days.

Pillows propped up, TV on, snacks aplenty, "me" time mama calls it. Earlier it was a tent with flashlights and ghost stories. It was a haven for four-legged Precious as she came scratching on the side of the bed seeking a refuge from those young bucks who flopped around in their bed, jeopardizing her life as her dog years accumulated.

In sickness, it's a clinic. Fresh sheets make it feel like a reward. In cold weather it's a warm cave when you pull the covers over your head. Sometimes it's a refuge from the world. Then sometimes it's the worst reminder of loneliness when the pillow across the giant divide lies unoccupied. You didn't change the last pillowcase. It smelled of him. Her perfume lingered on it. You can hold them close for a moment. You and your like-minded survivor friends know the battle. If you were younger you could have a sleepover. A lady I knew lived in an imposing mansion in our community and was known to spend the night with a good lady friend. Her almost unlimited resources couldn't make the lonely place any warmer.

Once again I'll lay my weary head on the pillow, grateful to say "I love you" and hear "Love you" back. I routinely used to say "Me, too" in response, but after catching a glimpse of Death's coat tail passing by my door, I figure it's worth it to put inhibition aside and say the full thing. "Love you, too." At least in the dark she can't see me blushing.

Real Prosperity

Commercial products constantly promote themselves as newer, better, stronger, improved, larger, more, and the list goes on. Food products are tastier, bigger, more flavorful, richer, creamier, and much more. We know advertisers are saying anything to get you to try old products again or use new products.

Even in the spiritual world you find something known as prosperity theology. The idea is that you can be materially prosperous by calling on a higher power to give you material wealth. Receipt of said wealth would supposedly reinforce or serve as evidence of the strength of your faith in the higher power. Some people quote James 4:2 that says, "You have not because you ask not." They imply that it is our fault because we don't have enough faith to get a higher power to give us stuff. They teach that if we just had a little more faith we would have great prosperity. Some people refer to Malachi 3:10 where we are urged to see "if I will not open you the windows of heaven, and pour you out a blessing, that there shall not be room enough to receive it." It sounds too good to be true. They say we don't have because we don't ask. A faith that implies that our faith must not be too strong since we don't have a lot of stuff has missed some important points.

How much stuff do we need? Is there something wrong with us if we don't want a bunch of stuff? The Lord's Prayer tells us to ask for our daily bread, not weekly, monthly, or yearly bread. It implies that we must be so close to our provider that we must depend on Him daily rather than checking in once in a while when we needed something special. Someone once told me that the only time his kids got in touch with him was when they needed something; he didn't have much daily contact with his children. A lot of us live that way spiritually, only checking in with God when we need something, maybe sounding a lot like Ray Stevens when he sings in his song, "It's me again, Margaret."

James 4:2 may say "you have not because you ask not," but it follows in verse 3 that "you ask and receive not, because you ask amiss, that you may consume it upon your lusts." This implies we cannot become prosperous just by asking. We also know that Malachi 3:10 and its promise to flood us with things is dependent on us bringing our tithes into the storehouse, something many of us fail to do.

It seems that we can have our material needs met by asking in a way that doesn't just give us stuff but also honors Him. One of those tests of faithfulness is that of tithes, giving back from our blessings. The blessings given us come to us when we obey God's directions. Life is about following directions, not necessarily connected to some evangelists who tell us we can become prosperous if we will just follow their directions. Sin is being disobedient. The prosperity that some people seek may not be in the best interests of someone who cannot handle it. What seems to work best in our lives is to follow the commandments of God and depend on Him for daily provision. God wrapped it up in Acts 11:13 when talking about Him providing for our needs, he asked, "If you then, being evil, know how to give good gifts unto your children, how much more shall your heavenly father give the Holy Spirit to them that ask him?" It seems like the key to real prosperity comes from having an actual relationship with a heavenly Father.

Don't Let It Fester

In Junior High we used to roll around at football practice in sand close to where the bus lot is now. There was this mean, thorny sticker called a goat head that didn't just stick, it hurt. Who hasn't made the mistake of getting into a patch of grassburrs? The one, however, that seemed to have the most lingering effect was something we called sticker weeds. Nobody wore shoes in the summertime which might explain stumped toes and missing toe nails. Worse still were the stupid stickers that got in our feet and had to be dug out. Most likely Mama would open up a safety pin, dig around, and hopefully remove the rascal. If not, sooner or later, it would fester up and eventually it would almost pop out on its own, much to our relief. Then the healing could begin.

Unfortunately for many of us we've got some of those places inside of us that just won't go away. They may have been there for years. They seem to fester up, aggravate us, and crawl back into their hole for a while. The sad truth is they are sores of our own making. We may not have caused them, but we haven't done anything to locate the emotional sticker and start the healing.

Bumper stickers proclaim that life happens. Recessions happen next door; depressions occur at your house. A world of people, both men and women, had some bad things forced upon them by family members and strangers. Through no fault of their own, good people are walking around with bad memories and emotional scars, many from childhood. Evil exists. Where was God when it all took place? He was there. The rain falls on the just and the unjust. The Devil may have done his best to wreck your life and leave you a bundle of nerves. It doesn't have to stop there.

Those festering stickers in your memory bank need to be pricked, drained, and healed. A little spiritual salve, maybe the balm of Gilead, needs to be applied. If you don't dredge those old memories up, you can't give them over to the Great Physician who can heal them. Take the power away from the source of the pain. When you forgive the offender, you take the last ounce of power from them. Even if they have gone to the grave, for your own sake you need to unburden that pain and tell the offender they no longer have power over you. As surely as Christ pulled the evil spirit from the demoniac in Gadarenes, so, too, can we get rid of that festering spirit affecting our relationships with others, our peace of mind, and even those cries in the night as we wake ourselves in the midst of nightly battles against old enemies. Hamlet said, "To sleep, perchance to dream." It's time to swap those bad dreams and nightmares for blessed sleep. The offenders have long forgotten or never knew the depth of pain they dealt you as they served only their selfish, sickly desires. Time to cut the cord and kick the sorry scum to the curb. No more power. Done. Turn it over to a healing force and let air into that dark room where until now only you have gone. Now what are you going to do with all that room in your heart and mind. How about grabbing a grandbaby or a sweet child, hold them close, and get busy making some new, sweeter memories.

A Little Sugar

Early in my administrative career a group of students did a play at my school. One of the characters was the principal, a man who spent a lot of his time constantly expressing gratitude to those around him. I don't really think I was that obvious, but apparently I did it enough to be apparent to those at my job.

I've always told people that you never get in trouble for doing a good deed; someone probably has but it's likely pretty rare. For me it just seems like you can't go wrong being kind and thankful in life, especially when you think about what all we have to be grateful for. Paul tells us in Thessalonians, "In everything give thanks: for this is the will of God in Christ Jesus concerning you."

I am not talking about touching the TV for the evangelist to get a financial blessing as some prosperity preachers espouse. If you have two customers come into your shop at the same time, and one is crabby and cold while the other is genuinely warm and expresses gratefulness for your help, which one do you want to help first? We love to be appreciated and thanked. This is one thing we can do that is cost effective and painless. As noted earlier, it lets us be momentarily spiritual when that may not be our general nature, unfortunately.

When you brag on the cake, the baker wants to make you another one. This is not meant to be phony like Eddie Haskell on Leave It To Beaver. It's common courtesy and common sense. When people feel appreciated, it happens so rarely that they will trip over themselves to wait on you and serve you. Money cannot replace the feeling we get when we feel that people value us. It makes us want to go the extra mile. It makes you want to put a little more product in their bucket to show how much you value being appreciated.

This makes us seem slightly childish, but part of us will always be childish. When Christ said, "Suffer the little children to come unto me," I like to believe He's including me, too. Much of what you and I have known as common courtesy is gone. Today most servers are not outdoing themselves to serve you. Look in the stores with a dozen cash registers and maybe 3 people checking you out. Find somebody in the aisle to help you. When you do find someone to help you, or you get that good server who goes the extra mile, some extra appreciation and a decent tip, aka 20% when appropriate, will go a long way toward getting you that great service the next time you stop in to the restaurant. After Christmas or Spring cleaning or shrub trimming, a couple of bucks taped to a trash bag can help ensure the guys in the big truck will be more likely to pick up all the extra sacks or limbs and best of all, do it with a smile. Everybody loves being appreciated.

The Battle

I once worked with a friend at the coal mine who was rougher than a cob. He helped train me to be a supervisor while spewing epithets that singed my hair. He made a profession of faith in Christ and totally changed. As people said of Scrooge in the movie, "He became as good a friend as could be found." He devoted the rest of his life to visiting prisons and living his faith daily.

Most of us have some degree of struggle or battle each day as we strive to implement faith into the struggle for control of our daily lives. Some people declare themselves to be nonbelievers and thus outwardly avoid the issue; however, most of us are somewhere on the scale of effectiveness in making faith a part of our lives. We know that even the Apostle Paul bemoaned his human failings when he said," I do not understand what I do. For what I want to do I do not do, but what I hate, I do." We all know about the lapses in faith of Peter, David, Abraham, Moses, and the list goes on. We're reminded that "To err is human, to forgive is divine."

Most of us spend our days battling the forces that want to totally destroy our lives while foolishly or stubbornly declining to call on a power source that could make the battle easier. We're told we battle not against humans but powers of darkness and principalities.

Anyone who has experienced or seen breakups of marriages and families can tell you about the powers of darkness that often "Go about as a roaring lion seeking whom he may devour." Watching normally good people become totally selfish "and to heck with anyone else" defies logic. It blows our mind to see people do things that you would never have predicted in a million years.

Somewhere in all our human messes pride has to play a role. Maybe we get too comfortable in our existence or too cocky in our abilities. We take the training wheels off and say "I can do it." I think we underestimate the strength and determination of the second most powerful force in the universe. As is the case of a lot of criminals, we get to thinking we are smarter than we are. The secret or key to at least holding your own in this daily battle is to acknowledge our weaknesses and call on that higher power for guidance. We're told "If my people who are called by my name will humble themselves, and pray and seek my face, and turn from their wicked ways, then will I hear from heaven, and will forgive their sin and heal their land."

That is a pretty clear roadmap to winning the daily battle all us weak believers face. A lot of stubborn people will ignore that admonition. I ask, "How's that working out for you?"

Dependable

I was taking out the trash one day when I looked over at the prince feathers that had come up with their purplish red heads. Call em coxcombs if you'd druther. Sure as it turned hot and dry, I knew they'd show up. If only people were as dependable as that.

A lot of us have been disappointed or hurt by people who promised to be a part of our lives but weren't. We're always being told that people will let us down sooner or later. It still hurts when they do. Grown people often carry parental divorce scars just beneath the surface long after the event.

A Hispanic lady friend told me what made a man sexy was having a job. Nothing glamorous about taking out the trash, but if I didn't, what would happen? Same thing goes for mowing the lawn, paying the bills, balancing the checkbook and a few other mini jobs I have. My wife has her list, too. Holding a job, keeping the house, in all these things we take each other for granted, but they come under the category of dependability. Not exciting or necessarily fun, but it's nice to know it's going to get done.

There's a world of people out there who haven't had the benefit of dependable people in their lives. What a lot of us take for granted as just part of our family role, they either lost or never had the luxury of that extra hand to help get things done. Some of us might yearn for a little pzazz while others would love to have just the basics. If you have it in your family relationships, you may take it for granted or overlook it. When you don't have those relationships now or ever, you may find yourself wishing for a trash taker outer or a lawn mowing partner.

Counting on others is often something we take for granted. A policeman was recently shot and killed; his child asked the mother if it meant they would have to move. Years ago a survey of teenagers found their greatest fear to be the loss of a parent. Maybe us humans should spend a little more time thinking about our family members and their impact on our lives.

People who are part of a traditional family hitting on all cylinders may not truly appreciate or fully value what they are a part of. Those who have not been blessed with the stable home of dependable people often become doubly motivated to make that a goal in future relationships. Make lemons into lemonade. Maybe it's time to give thanks for the blessing of a dependable family. If you don't have one, give thanks for what you do have and if possible take the steps necessary to help build or strengthen them to what you desire in a family relationship.

Extra Mile

An older successful friend once volunteered his secret to success. He called it, "And Then Some." Anyone who knows me or have read my books Serving Happiness and Class Rules, know that I believe the secret to happiness is serving others. This new motto would also work because in serving others and not yourself, the bigger the serving, the happier you and the recipient will be. Luke 6:38 says, "Give, and it will be given to you. A good measure, pressed down, shaken together and running over, will be poured into your lap. For with the measure you use, it will be measured to you."

Think about your favorite places to eat. The Fish Fry in Paris has built a great reputation for quality, quantity, and speedy service. At the Borderline Café in Powderly, whatever size steak you order will end up being bigger than you ordered and will be gooood. Burgers and Fries in Sulphur Springs will load you up with big fries and a big burger. Fatboy's BBQ in Cooper will give you ample portions of awesome ribs and delish onion rings. South Main Café in Paris will cover your plate in bacon, biscuits and gravy, hash browns, fried eggs and do it with a smile.

I've always told people that I meet that the key to keeping a job and advancement is making yourself indispensable, not scarce. When the layoffs come, you'll be the last to go. When the raises come, you'll be the first in line. If you do your job and then some, they will love you. Even at 18 I busted my tail heading up a sheetrock crew for a builder from out of town. The next thing I know I'm called into the office and offered a great opportunity to promote and travel. Another company owned by my friends pulled me on a cold morning to tell me I could work for them any time I was home from college. I think I was scooping up stray concrete chunks in freezing weather at the time.

The idea of serving others and going the extra mile is complemented with an accompanying smile. People who are optimistic and positive in outlook are contagious. They brighten up the whole place. You get paid the same, crabby or kind, but one's attitude makes all the difference. I always loved it when visitors would come to my building and compliment us on having a great working climate. Attitude starts at the top. My wife once asked me why I only hired good looking employees. I jokingly told her I'm the one who has to look at the scenery all day; it might as well be pleasant. You'll spend more time there than at home. For a great work atmosphere serve others, go the extra mile, and above all, smile.

Getting By With A Little Help From Your Friends

Tim McGraw had a really great song called "Always Be Humble and Kind." No one has to tell you how hard it is to do that. Lubbock's own Mac Davis used to strut around in tight jeans singing "Oh Lord it's hard to be humble when you're perfect in every way." Humility is almost impossible to maintain while living in isolation from others. Even the monks and nuns have someone to appropriately help keep them humble.

Since I had no inclination to live a cloistered life, I've tried to do the next best thing. I found by getting involved with others, especially those operating under the umbrella of an organized faith or spiritual foundation where I could serve others and be around people to help keep me in line. At Tech I found support at the Baptist Student Union, in my college dept. at First Baptist Lubbock, and more individually through Campus Crusade for Christ out of Colorado Springs. My buddy and I routinely visited other colleges in places like Odessa and Canyon to interact with and encourage other college students.

The military was instrumental in putting me on the Canadian border where I got to be a part of the Billy Graham Crusade and serve as a counselor for them at Marquette. While there I got to help build a new church building in the Upper Peninsula of Michigan complete with numb fingers and toes as the cold air blew in off Lake Superior. Its waters were so cold we lost a B-52 crew patrolling against Russian intrusion in those icy waters that don't yield up any bodies. Speaking of bodies, I found a few there. While I spent my spare time trout and salmon fishing, dipping smelt, ice fishing, skiing, snow shoeing, playing ball for the Air Force, other airmen chose not to do anything but dope. The long winters of isolation created more than a few addicts. I put on an additional duty of drug prevention officer as we tried to salvage addicts before the military kicked them out to survive or die in the real world.

Europe and the Middle East were exciting times for a single guy. I served as the youth pastor for Hahn Baptist Church in Germany and sponsored youth trips to Paris, Spain, Austria, and Switzerland with the AYA youth center on base. A friend of mine and African American lay preacher helped us form a worship group that met in meadows in the shadow of old castles in the Rhine Valley. In town we found an old house and added bunk beds for 30. It became our outreach to the heroin addicts and hash smokers who wanted to get off the stuff. I made friends with the grocery sackers at our military commissary. They were known as the Navigators out of Colorado. Once discharged from the military they stayed in Germany to share a house and minister one-on-one to young Christians. They were kind enough to take me in and spend time helping reinforce my faith.

What I've discovered is that if you look for something you will find it. I sought people who could help me stay grounded and make a difference in people's lives. It really is true, "Seek and ye shall find." Time is short. Paul's admonition is even more relevant today than ever. Ephesians 5:16 admonishes us, "Redeeming the time, because the days are evil."

People Are Crazy

Ten years or so ago Billy Currington had a hit record where the hook was, "God is great, beer is good, and people are crazy." Most of us could settle on two out of three. I venture to say most of us run into a few crazy people every now and then. Some of them may not even be in your family.

People never cease to amaze me. I like to eat by myself or sit in an airport and watch folks. They all have a story. I try to figure out what it might be. Things have gotten less interesting since the smart phone arrived. What's so smart about a phone that keeps you from talking to family and friends across the table from you at Whataburger. I wonder if we could ever go back to just sitting with friends and watching their faces. Most communication is not words but body language and people's eyes. Any man will tell you that you're in deep dodo when you get that look from Sweetie. No text message can replace it.

Crazy people say, "I drank a six pack last night." It obviously wasn't coke, and you couldn't be that thirsty. Maybe you just like running to the john! Crazy people get out on the streets and highways and get in conflicts with people they don't know over some slight as they were driving. Ordinarily semi-sane people sometimes go bonkers behind the wheel. When I drove in Germany I figured the unlimited speeds on their interstates called autobahns helped them relieve the stress of losing the two wars to us. Either way you learned to get out of the way. That finger to the temple in Italy did not represent their IQ, although it could be their driving IQ as you hit intersections packed with cars.

Crazy people develop a strong attachment to things, more so than to people. Relationships take a back seat. They have a hard time grasping the concept of leaving this earth at some point. If you seriously understood that you can't take it with you, and you're wife is going to practically give it away at a garage sale, would you spend a little more time with people instead of things?

I like a pretty yard, but not enough to mow it three times a week. I watch people obsessed with their lawns and their sometime testy relationships with neighbors. They rarely have a visitor, and don't appear to be bothered by that. Sometime later I've walked by their room in the nursing home. I wanted to tell em about the new owner parking on the grass and dripping oil on the driveway. Crazy people realize too late what matters. It ain't the lawn of the month or the stuff you'll leave behind.

Filling Their Spot

I was on a job the other day when an old friend and sometime customer stopped by. Since we are Christians, we didn't gossip, but we "shared" a few thoughts about others. It dawned on me that she is still full of vim and vigor as she approaches ninety years of age. I tell her she is my hero just because I want to look that good and be that alert when I'm her age.

Another friend from church has passed ninety and maintains his walking schedule every day. I've watched him walk as he comes by my job sites; I wouldn't want to have to keep up with him. He tells me he has a hard time hearing in church. I'm kinda jealous because I don't have a good excuse to not listen when my wife starts telling me about her redecorating plans.

Another little lady from church up in her 90's has finally been told she might need to turn over the car keys and pick up a cane. Until lately I couldn't keep up with her. She has been a daily caregiver to her brother and sister in the nursing home. Mercifully the sister just passed, and the brother may have to be hospitalized to have a procedure done. God granted my friend the strength to help her siblings in their last days even though she had passed 90.

Just as we're seeing the passing of our WWII vets who are shrinking in number, so, too, are those senior saints we've counted on in church and in our community. I'm not sure I see others taking their place. They have been so faithful and dependable in their duties of looking out for the others in their group at church and in the community. Just looking at the shrinking numbers in their section at church, I'm not that confident we can find suitable replacements. Oh, that's right.

We are the replacements. Pogo the cartoon character once said," We have found the enemy and he is us." If our faithful numbers are shrinking at church and elsewhere, maybe we are the reason. It's hard to accept and understand that I'm acquiring a new role and new duties these days. Mentally I often think I'm still 30 until my left hip goes sideways and reminds me to add 40.

The cycle of life is so gradual that is sneaks up on you. One day it bites you in the rear. Not long ago I was watching those older folks struggle to get up and out of the pew. Today I think I have become my own grandpa. Be nice. You'll get there soon enough.

52120484R00151

Made in the USA
Middletown, DE
07 July 2019